THE TOTAL ROCK BASSIST

>> A Fun and Comprehensive Overview of Rock Bass Playing

DAN BENNETT

Alfred, the leader in educational publishing,

and the National Guitar Workshop,

one of America's finest guitar schools, have joined

forces to bring you the best, most progressive

educational tools possible. We hope you will enjoy

this book and encourage you to look for

other fine products from Alfred and the

National Guitar Workshop.

Alfred Publishing Co., Inc.
16320 Roscoe Blvd., Suite 100
P.O. Box 10003
Van Nuys, CA 91410-0003
alfred.com

ISBN-10: 0-7390-5269-1 (Book & CD)
ISBN-13: 978-0-7390-5269-3 (Book & CD)

This book was acquired, edited and produced
by Workshop Arts, Inc., the publishing arm of
the National Guitar Workshop.
Nathaniel Gunod, acquisitions, managing editor
Burgess Speed, senior editor
Matthew Liston, editor
Timothy Phelps, interior design and photography
Ante Gelo, music typesetter
CD recorded by Mark Schane-Lydon at WorkshopLive.com, Pittsfield, MA
CD mastered by Collin Tilton at Bar None Studio, Northford, CT
Dan Bennett (bass), Pete Sweeney (drums), Raleigh Green (guitar)

Cover photograph: © JUPITERIMAGES / Creatas / Alamy
Bass on cover courtesy Schecter Guitars.

Table of Contents

About the Author

Dan Bennett has been playing bass guitar and other instruments for over 10 years. He received a Bachelor's in Music Performance, with special emphasis in Music Business, from the University of Massachusetts Lowell. Dan has played in many groups in various styles such as progressive metal, hardcore, punk, pop-rock, indie/alt rock, jazz, and more. He has toured the country and has spent hundreds of hours in the studio with these bands.

Dan currently works for the online music education Website WorkshopLive.com and also teaches privately. Dan is the primary author of the *Sample CD Marketing Plan*, a book published through Music Business Solutions (www.mbsolutions.com).

Photo by Timothy Phelps

Acknowledgements

Thanks to my bass mentors: Rudi Weeks for constantly grilling me on my technique and exposing me to a vast array of styles; and Mark Henry for expanding my knowledge and application of music theory as well as constantly challenging my abilities on the bass guitar. Thanks to Tim Brault and Scott Drapeau for being my musical cohorts for so long, and always helping me to push the musical envelope. Thanks to Burgess Speed and Nat Gunod for giving me the opportunity to write this book; Tim Phelps and Matthew Liston for their work on it; and of course, to Pete Sweeney and Raleigh Green for playing on the CD. Thanks to my friends and family for constantly supporting my musical endeavors, and to anyone and everyone I have had the pleasure of creating music with.

Introduction

The bass guitar is the youngest of the core instruments in rock music. As rock music has evolved over the past 50 or so years, the art of playing the bass guitar has evolved as well.

The intention of *The Total Rock Bassist* is to do more than just show you a few licks and tricks; it is to teach you the theory behind them, as well as the vast array of styles that make up rock bass playing. This book will explore the role of the bass player in some of the most popular rock styles. You'll learn about the relationship a bassist needs to have with the other instruments, so that you can enhance the overall sound of the band. You'll also be exposed to ideas and concepts in music theory that have been used in rock and many other styles of music as well.

However, theory is not law, and what has worked for others in the past might not work for you. Rock music has always been about being different and rebellious. While studying the theory and techniques of those who have come before you will certainly benefit your playing ability, I encourage you to constantly explore new ideas.

The Total Rock Bassist is intended for players of all ability levels. No previous experience is required to use this book. If you are an absolute beginner, you will find a clear explanation of basic skills such as holding the bass, tuning, reading standard music notation and TAB, and right- and left-hand technique. Even if you are an experienced player, you will find challenging examples to expand your horizons.

When rock 'n' roll first came about in the 1950s, the music had a particular sound; but, today, rock music encompasses thousands of sub-genres and is influenced by all kinds of music. New genres and styles are constantly being innovated, like rap metal, gypsy punk, hardcore bluegrass, and much more. This proves that music has no rules and no boundaries. The ideas, techniques, and styles in this book are only a fraction of what you can do. Learn these ideas, but remember that they are just that, ideas. Go out and find or create your own voice.

In regards to learning an instrument and practicing, I'll leave you with a quote from the great jazz saxophonist Charlie Parker that sums up what I'm trying to say:

"Music is your own experience, your own thoughts, your wisdom. If you don't live it, it won't come out of your [bass]. They teach you there's a boundary line to music. But, man, there's no boundary line to art."

A compact disc is available with this book. Using the disc will help make learning more enjoyable and the information more meaningful. Listening to the CD will help you correctly interpret the rhythms and feel of each example. The symbol to the left appears next to each song or example that is performed on the CD. Example numbers are above the symbol. The track number below each symbol corresponds directly to the song or example you want to hear. In some cases, there is more than one example per track; this is reflected in the track numbers (for example: track 2.1, track 2.2, track 2.3, etc.). Track 1 will help you tune to this CD.

Chapter 1: Getting Started

Parts of the Bass

An important part of playing any instrument is familiarizing yourself with its anatomy. Knowing about the various bits and pieces of the bass guitar will help you understand explanations of technique, as well as how to approach any possible problems you may encounter with your bass. Musical technology is constantly evolving, and many bass guitars have unique looks and sounds to them, but all have the same basic parts as illustrated in the diagram below.

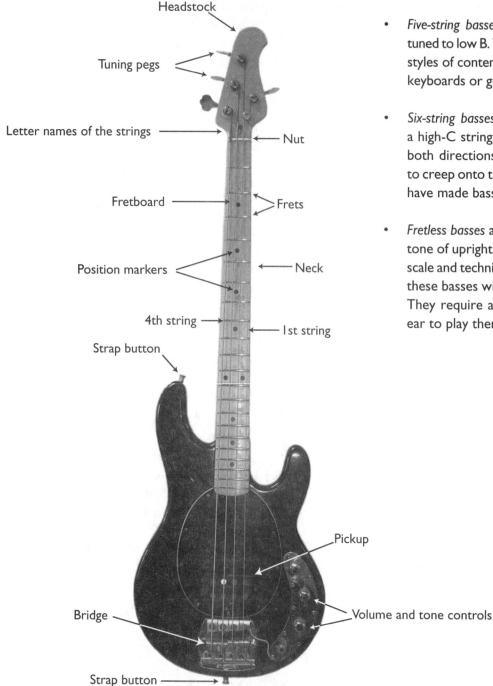

Headstock

Tuning pegs

Letter names of the strings

Nut

Fretboard

Frets

Position markers

Neck

4th string

1st string

Strap button

Pickup

Bridge

Volume and tone controls

Strap button

Different Types of Basses

The bass guitar is a fairly young instrument (compared to, say, the guitar or piano), with its origins in the late 1930s. The first mass-produced electric bass guitar was the Fender Precision Bass, which set the standard for the modern bass, with four strings, 20 frets, magnetic pickups, and a bolt-on neck. Today, the bass guitar has evolved greatly, and as bassists, we now have many different basses to choose from, each one serving a different purpose. Here are just a few common examples:

- *Five-string basses* feature an extra string, generally tuned to low B. Their lower range is helpful for certain styles of contemporary music, or when playing with keyboards or guitars that are tuned down.

- *Six-string basses* generally have a low-B string and a high-C string, extending the range of the bass in both directions. Seven-string basses are beginning to creep onto the market as well, and some builders have made basses with even more strings!

- *Fretless basses* are designed to emulate the feel and tone of upright, or double, basses, but maintain the scale and technique of the electric bass. You may see these basses with or without fret lines or markers. They require a great deal of accuracy and a good ear to play them properly.

Holding the Bass

Comfort is a factor that is often overlooked. Bad habits can easily result in strain and tension, which can be a problem when trying to execute certain techniques. The best place to start developing good habits is the way you hold your instrument. So, let's look at proper ways of holding the bass, both while sitting and standing.

Sitting with the Bass Guitar

The picture to the right shows the most common way to play while sitting. Be sure to hold the bass close to your body. This will ensure that you won't have to bend over the instrument to watch your fingers move along the fretboard. Also, notice how the neck of the instrument is at a slight upwards angle. The bodies of most bass guitars are shaped in ways that work well in this position.

Correct sitting position.

"Classical Guitar" Sitting Position

This is a less intuitive sitting position, but is very comfortable and makes reaching notes all over the fretboard very easy. You want to be sure to sit on the edge of your chair, holding the bass close to your body with the bass in between your legs (see right).

"Classical guitar" sitting position.

Standing with the Bass Guitar

Very rarely do rock bassists sit when playing gigs, so be sure to invest in a comfortable and adjustable strap. When you stand, you want the bass to be in almost the same position it would be in if you were sitting (see right). There have been many bassists who hurt themselves or their playing ability by slinging the bass extra low (see below left), or, in some cases, extra high (see below right) in order to look "cool." While some bassists do get away with this, you should practice wearing the bass at a medium height at first and then find a position that works best for your own style.

Correct way to hold the bass while standing.

Bass too low.

Bass too high.

Right- and Left-Hand Technique

Each finger of the right and left hand is assigned a number, as shown in the photos to the right. These numbers will be useful abbreviations as we discuss left- and right-hand technique throughout the book.

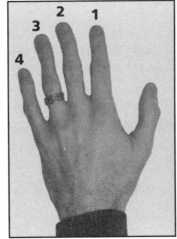
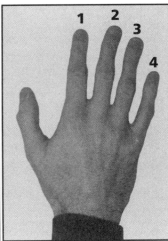

Fingers of the left hand.   *Fingers of the right hand.*

Right-Hand Position

The right hand is primarily in charge of your rhythmic technique. For the majority of the exercises in this book, you will be using the 1st and 2nd fingers of your right hand to pluck the strings. (There are some exercises, however, that are designed to be played with a pick.) Notice that your right-hand thumb can be anchored on either the pickups or the 4th string (only when it is not being played). (See photos below.)

Thumb anchored on pickup.

Thumb anchored on the 4th string.

Left-Hand Position

Bad left-hand position can be another source of tension for bassists. You want to make sure your thumb is positioned in the middle of the neck, behind the 2nd finger. You want to keep your wrist and forearm as straight as possible. A slight curve is okay, but don't let it get out of control. If you are practicing and feel some tension, you should shake out your arm, let it drop naturally to your side, and allow your fingers to relax. Slowly, bring it back up to the neck, and the natural, relaxed curve of your fingers will put you in proper playing position.

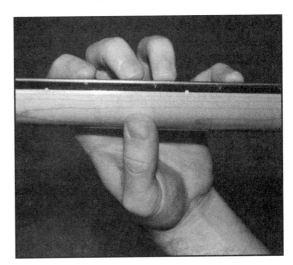

Correct left-hand position.

Tuning

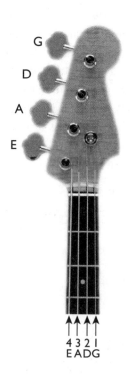

In order from thickest, or lowest-sounding, to the thinnest, or highest-sounding, the strings on the bass guitar are labeled with the numbers 4, 3, 2, and 1. Each string also has a letter name, which is the name of the note that sounds when the string is played open. From lowest to highest, the note names of the strings are E, A, D, and G (see right).

Keeping your instrument in tune is essential to sounding your best. It is unfortunate that bass players have become notorious for being out of tune. (Did you ever hear the one about the bassist who was so out of tune, even *he* noticed?) So, let's fight this stereotype and learn how to keep the instrument in tune both with itself and with the other instruments with which you'll be playing.

Electronic Tuners

The easiest way to tune your bass is with an *electronic tuner* (see photo below). There are a wide variety of electronic tuners, ranging in price from $15 to $200. They all basically do the same thing, but some have different features, such as *pedal tuners*, which are great to have on stage, or *rack tuners*, which attach directly to your amplifier. Some tuners even have a built-in *metronome*, which is an essential tool to help you keep time.

For most bass players, an inexpensive electronic tuner works just fine. All you need to do is plug a standard ¼" cable from your bass into the tuner, play an open string, and the tuner should tell you what note you are playing and whether or not that string is *sharp* (too high) or *flat* (too low). The tuner will have an indicator (in the form of lights or a needle) that moves from side to side. When the string is flat, the indicator will point to the left; if the string is sharp, the indicator will point to the right. Use the tuning machines to make the adjustments until the indicator is exactly in the middle.

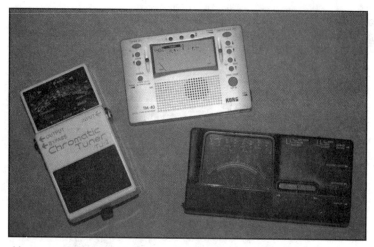

Various electronic tuners.

Relative Tuning

Another method of tuning is called *relative tuning*. This method allows you to make sure all the strings on your bass are in tune with each other, without using an electronic tuner. You might not necessarily be tuned to *A440* (the tuning standard used by most musicians and electronic tuners), but you will sound in tune with yourself and the other musicians with whom you are playing. Here's how it works:

Step 1. First, tune your open 4th string (E) to a piano, keyboard, pitch pipe, or your guitarist's low-E string. On a keyboard, use the E that is 19 white keys below middle C (see diagram below).

Step 2. Play the 5th fret of the 4th string, and then play the open 3rd string. These two notes should sound identical, as they are both the note A. If not, tune the 3rd string so that it matches the pitch of the 5th fret of the 4th string. Adjust the pitch up (if the string is flat) or down (if the string is sharp).

Step 3. To tune your 2nd string, place a finger on the 5th fret of the 3rd string to produce the note D. The open 2nd string should match this note. If not, use the tuning peg for the 2nd string to adjust it up (if the string is flat) or down (if the string is sharp).

Step 4. To tune your 1st string, place a finger on the 5th fret of the 2nd string to produce the note G. The open 1st string should match this note. If not, use the tuning peg for the 1st string to adjust it up (if the string is flat) or down (if the string is sharp).

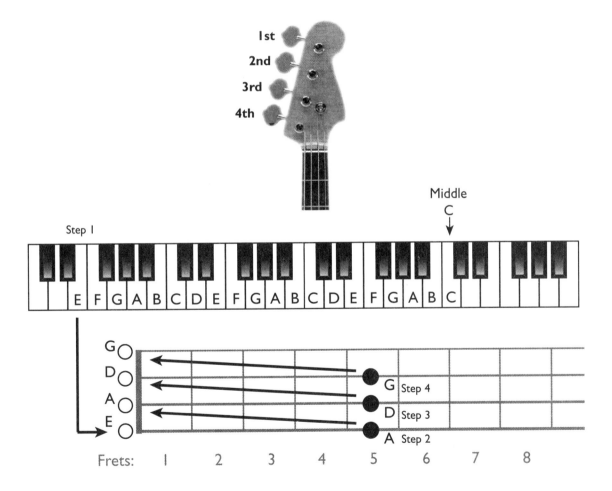

Strings

There are many reasons why different types of bass guitar strings sound different. Strings come in various *gauges* or thicknesses. Thinner strings are often easier for beginners to play and have a brighter sound, while thicker strings tend to have a beefier tone. There are three main types of *windings* for bass guitar strings: *round-wound*, *flat-wound*, and *half-flat*. Each type has its own distinctive feel and sound. Round-wound strings feel somewhat rough under your fingers, due to the many windings. They have the brightest, most aggressive sound, but are prone to finger noise as you move your hand around. Flat-wound strings have the windings flattened so that they feel smooth and do not generate as much finger noise. They have a deep, mellow sound. Half-flat strings are a compromise between the two.

Changing the Strings

After much playing, strings wear out and sound "dead." Although bass strings are thicker than normal guitar strings, they do break, and it's always a good idea to have a spare set of strings around. Following are instructions for changing a string on the bass. (Also see photos to the right.) If you are changing all the strings, follow these directions for each string.

1. Loosen the string by turning the tuning machine clockwise (there are rare occasions where a bass may have reverse-thread tuning machines, and you will need to tune the opposite direction).

2. Pull the string through the bridge.

3. Insert the new string through the bridge, pull tightly across neck, and cut off any excess string about two inches past that string's tuning machine.

4. Insert the string in the string post and twist it around the post in a clockwise fashion.

5. Then, turn the tuning machine counter-clockwise and tune up that string.

Stretching the Strings

New strings will always go out of tune much more easily than older strings, and the reason for this is that the older strings have been stretched over time from playing and tuning.

A way to avoid having to constantly tune your new strings is to stretch them once they are on your bass. An effective way to do this is to first tune all the strings to the correct pitch. Then, take one string, pull it out as far as it can go, and let it snap back into place (see right); do this about three times and then re-tune that string. Repeat this process until the stretching no longer causes the string to go out of tune. Do this with all of your strings, and you will find that your bass stays in tune much longer.

1.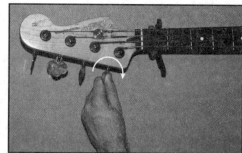

2.

3.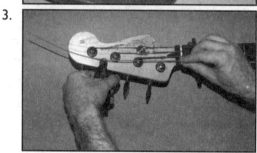

4.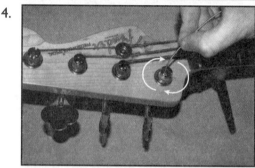

5.

Stretching the strings.

Chapter 2: Reading Music Notation

Although many rock musicians have had success without ever knowing how to read a single note of standard music notation, it is a valuable skill to have. It will give you more options for expressing yourself and your music. Being able to read music will also help to give you a better understanding of what you are playing and the music you are hearing. Plus, if you can read music, you have a better chance of getting paying gigs, or even being hired as a studio musician.

Pitch

Pitch refers to how low or high a note sounds. Each pitch is represented by a *note*. Notes vary in how they look; some are open circles, some are filled, and some have stems and flags.

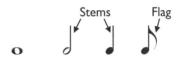

Staff

Notes are written on what we call a *staff*. The staff is made up of five lines and four spaces. Notes fall either upon a line or within a space. The shape at the beginning of the staff is known as the *clef*. Bassists use the *bass clef* shown below, which is also known as the *F clef*.

The Staff

Bass clef

Note Names

The *musical alphabet* consists of the first seven letters of the English alphabet (A–B–C–D–E–F–G). Each line or space on the staff represents a different pitch. There are easy ways, like the sayings below, to remember which pitches fall on which space or line. The first letter of each word represents a pitch.

Certain notes fall below or above the staff; *ledger lines* are used to indicate these pitches.

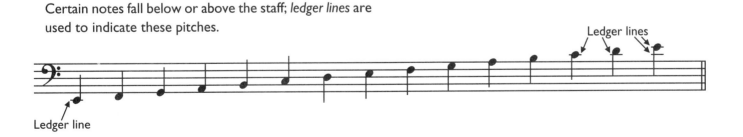

Musical Time

Beats and Measures

When we play music, the timing is guided by what we call the *beat*, which is our musical unit of time. The beat is the driving pulse of the music.

We organize groups of notes on the staff into *measures,* or *bars.* The vertical lines shown on the staff are *barlines* and indicate when a measure ends or begins. *Double barlines* indicate the end of a piece or section.

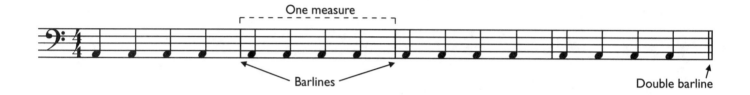

Patterns of sounds and silences—made up of notes and *rests* of different "values"—are known as *rhythms.* Before we start playing the Rhythmic Exercises on page 16, we need to take a look at these different note and rest values.

Note Values

We know that the location of the note on the staff dictates the pitch of the note. Likewise, the appearance of a note dictates its *value,* or how long it lasts. (This is also referred to as the *duration* of a note.) Below is a breakdown of the different kinds of notes and how long each one is played for.

Note Values

Whole Note	= 4 beats
Half Notes	= 2 beats each
Quarter Notes	= 1 beat each
Eighth Notes	= ½ beat each
Sixteenth Notes	= ¼ beat each

Rest Values

The symbols for *rests* represent musical silence. These are counted the same way as their corresponding note values, and break down the same way. Being able to play rests accurately is just as important as playing notes.

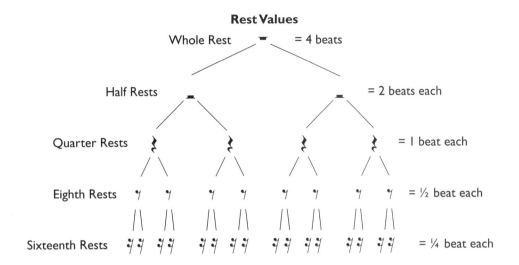

Rest Values

Time Signatures

At the beginning of each piece, after the clef, is a set of numbers, one on top of the other. This is called the *time signature,* and it tells us how many beats occur in each measure. The top number represents how many beats occur in the measure, and the bottom number tells which kind of note receives one beat.

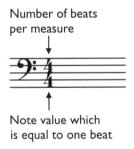

So in $\frac{4}{4}$ time, you have four beats to the measure, and the quarter note receives one beat. This means you can have any combination of note values and rest values within a measure, as long as they add up to four beats. The beats of a measure are counted in the following way.

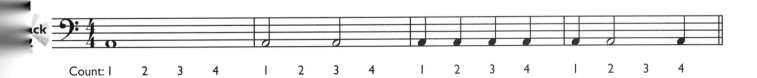

Rhythmic Exercises

These exercises will help you get used to reading different rhythmic note and rest values. They feature a combination of whole notes, half notes, and quarter notes. Each exercise will be in $\frac{4}{4}$ time, so be sure to count the beats aloud. You may also want to use a metronome, which is a tool that keeps time with a click. You can adjust the speed of the count, which is called the *tempo*, to match the tempo marking on the page (see example below).

When you hear someone count off "1, 2, 3, 4," or the drummer click his sticks before the song starts, they are setting the tempo of the song. If the tempo seems too fast, set the metronome to a slower tempo and build these exercises up to speed. All these examples can be played on the open 3rd string (A), but feel free to play these rhythms on any note you choose. Even if you can't fully read standard music notation, you should be able to read rhythms. As a bassist, interpreting rhythms is one of your most important jobs, so being able to accurately execute these exercises now, at the beginning stages of your bass playing, will make things much easier in the future. You'll see that the other form of music notation (*tablature*, or TAB) does not indicate rhythms, which is why being able to read rhythms is so important.

The example below uses three note values you should become very familiar with: whole notes, half notes, and quarter notes. When playing quarter notes, you want to use a technique called *alternate picking*. This means to either alternate between the 1st and 2nd fingers of your right hand, or if using a pick, alternate between picking up and down.

When you see the ⊓ symbol, use your 1st finger, or pluck down. The V symbol tells you to use your 2nd finger, or pluck upwards. Sometimes you may see a 1 or a 2 above the music to indicate which finger to pick with. You will not always see these written in future chapters, because alternate picking should eventually become second nature to you as a bassist.

⊓ = Use 1st finger to pluck string (or *downstroke*, if using pick)

V = Use 2nd finger to pluck string (or *upstroke*, if using pick)

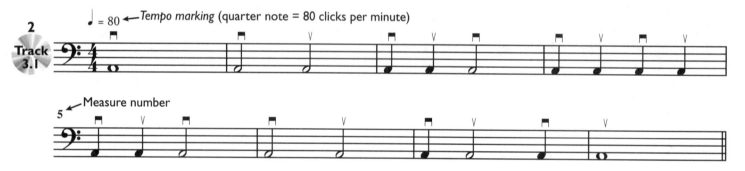

This next example will use half rests. To accurately execute the musical silence, you must stop the string from ringing. With an open string you can quickly, but gently, rest your left hand on the fretboard with just enough pressure to stop the string without pressing the strings down to the fretboard. With a fretted note, you can just lift your left-hand fingers off the fretboard, while still maintaining contact with the string.

The focus of this rhythmic exercise is quarter rests.

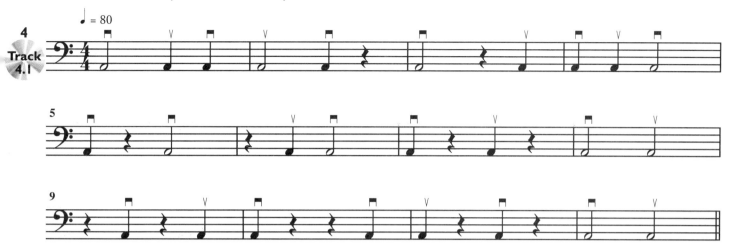

The focus of the following exercise is also quarter rests.
Be careful counting whenever you see two quarter rests
back to back, especially between measures.

This next example uses all three forms of rests: whole
rests, half rests, and quarter rests. Be sure to count aloud
and be patient when counting through these rests; keep
the tempo steady.

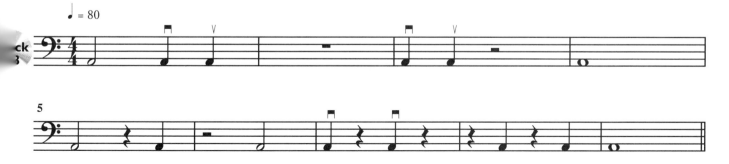

Tablature (TAB)

Another form of music notation is *tablature*, or *TAB* for short. The TAB staff has four lines representing the four strings of the bass. The lowest line represents the lowest string, E, and the highest line represents the highest string, G. The numbers that fall on these lines are the fret numbers to be played. A "0" represents a note that is an open string. The numbers underneath the TAB represent the left-hand finger to be used.

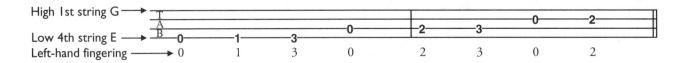

High 1st string G →

Low 4th string E →

Left-hand fingering →

All examples in this book will be presented in both standard music notation and TAB. Many guitarists and bass players have come to only read TAB, but compared to standard musical notation, TAB is limited. The most basic forms of TAB do not give any sort of rhythmic values to the notes, and this means you need to hear the piece of music before being able to play it. TAB also maps out the exact locations of where your fingers are supposed to fall on the fretboard. In standard music notation, however, the same pitch can be found in multiple locations on the instrument; it becomes the player's choice as to where he or she wishes to play that pitch. However, there are certain situations where TAB is very helpful. Take the time to become familiar with reading both TAB and standard music notation.

Chord Symbols

Often, your bass lines will follow a chord progression that is being played by a guitarist or keyboard player. To represent these chord progressions, we write *chord symbols* above the music. *Chords* are made up of three or more pitches being played simultaneously, and these symbols tell us which chords are being played, at what time. Your bass lines will most likely use notes taken from these chords, like in the example below. Later in the book, you'll learn how to more accurately read these chord symbols.

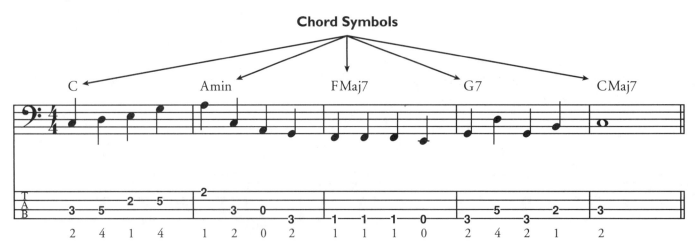

Finding Notes on the Fretboard

To apply pitches to the bass, look at the map of the bass fretboard below. This shows the neck of the bass up to the 12th fret, with the location of each note of the musical alphabet (A–B–C–D–E–F–G). You may notice that most note names are two frets apart, while the pitches of B and C, as well as E and F, are only one fret apart. The distance of one fret on the bass is a *half step*, and the distance of two frets is a *whole step*.

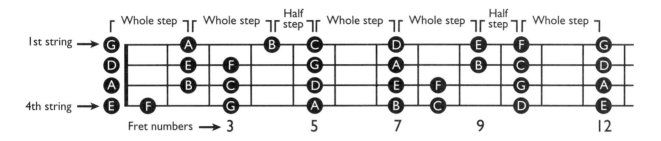

Accidentals

There are pitches in between the notes that are two frets apart. To understand how these pitches are named, you need to understand the concept of *accidentals*. Accidentals are symbols that alter the pitch of a note. They raise or lower the pitch of the note for the entire measure in which they appear.

Flats

A *flat* sign ♭ lowers the pitch by a half step. For example, if you saw a D in the music (which could be played on the 3rd string, 5th fret) with this symbol next to it, it would be called D-flat or D♭, and you would play it on the 3rd string, 4th fret.

Sharps

A *sharp* sign ♯ raises the pitch by a half step. For example, if you saw the same D note with this symbol, it would be called D-sharp or D♯ and could be played on the 3rd string, 6th fret.

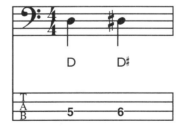

Naturals

A *natural* sign ♮ cancels a previous sharp or flat. There are certain *keys* (see page 29) that require you to always play a certain flat or sharp note; a natural sign would cancel this out for the measure in which it appears.

Enharmonic Notes

Enharmonic equivalents are notes with the same pitch but different names. For example, there is a whole step, or two frets, between the pitches of C and D. If the C is raised a half step, or made sharp, it is played as C♯. If the D is lowered, or made flat, it becomes D♭. Both of these notes are the same pitch, and played on the same fret, between notes C and D. When we play in an ascending fashion, going upwards in pitch, we name the pitches with sharps, and when descending, or going down in pitch, we name them using flats.

Check out the following map of the bass fretboard. It shows the location of every note up to the 12th fret, including both the natural and enharmonic (sharp and flat) notes.

Open strings

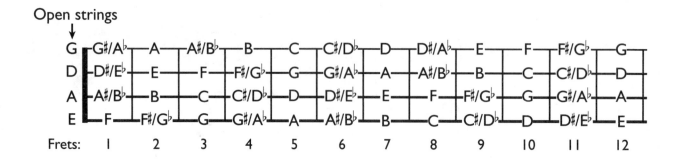

You may have also noticed that the same note names appear in different locations on the fretboard. Some of these pitches are exactly the same (like the A played on the 4th string at the 5th fret, and the open 3rd string A). Others are *octaves* (like the E played on the 4th string at the 12th fret, and the open 4th string E). An octave is the distance of 12 half steps between two notes with the same name.

The example below illustrates that there are 12 frets, or 12 half steps, in one octave. When we play the 12 half steps of an octave in order like this, it is called a *chromatic scale*.

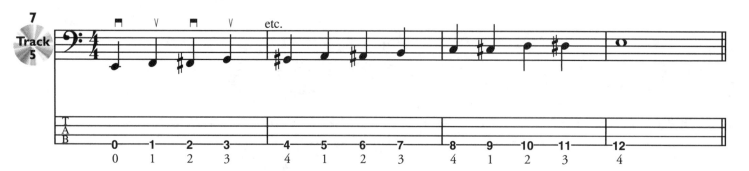

Memorizing the Fretboard

An excellent way to be able to read music and play it quickly is to memorize where the notes fall on your instrument. A good warm-up exercise is to focus on memorizing all the different locations of one note name on the fretboard. Memorize not only where they are, but where their respective pitches fall on the staff.

The following example shows a way to approach this exercise. Pay attention to both the standard music notation (which tells you where the pitch falls on the staff), and the TAB (which tells you what string and fret to play on). Be sure to say the note name aloud as you play it, and play all the locations one string at a time. This example starts with the open 4th string (E), and shows the location for all of the E notes up to the 12th fret. Although this example only shows four notes (E, F, F♯, and G), you should complete this chart on a separate piece of paper, and make sure to include all pitches. Remember, even though F♯ and G♭ have the same pitch and fret location, they are written differently on the staff.

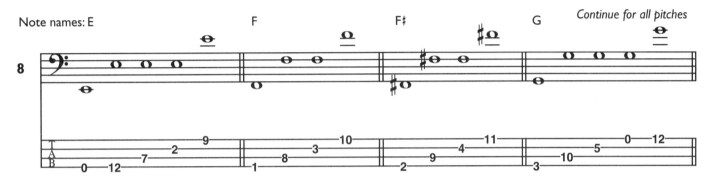

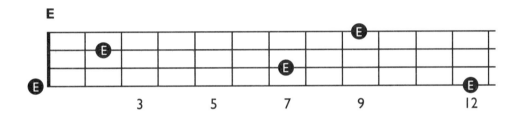

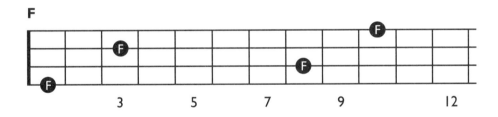

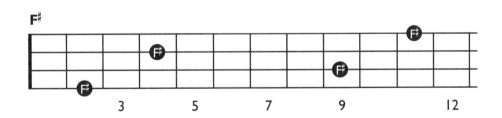

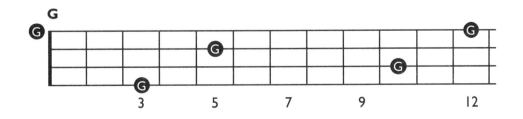

Finger Strengthening Warm-Up

Playing the bass is a physical activity as much as it is musical. Like most physical activities, it's always a good idea to stretch and do warm-ups. The following exercise is meant to be done as accurately as possible in order to help build strength and flexibility in both hands. The exercise moves up and down the chromatic scale on all four strings.

Try to hold down each finger on its note even after the next finger has played. For example, if your 4th finger is down on the 4th fret, try to keep your 1st, 2nd, and 3rd fingers on their frets. This may be difficult at first, but with time it will become easier.

Although the exercise is notated in quarter notes, to work on your right-hand technique, practice using different rhythmic values for each position. For example, start going up from the 4th string to the 1st string, playing each pitch as a whole note, then when coming down from the 1st string to the 4th string, play each pitch as a half note, then, when going back up play quarters, etc.

Chapter 3: The Major Scale

Major Scale Construction

The *major scale* is one of the most important parts of music theory, or the study of the mechanics of music. This is because much of the music theory you will be learning in the future is either derived from, or related to the major scale. It is very important that you not only learn how to play the major scale, but also understand how it's built and how it sounds. Everyone from the Beatles to Led Zeppelin has used the major scale.

The major scale follows a set pattern of whole steps and half steps from one pitch to an octave above that pitch. Using the C Major scale, from the notes C to C, the pattern is whole step, whole step, half step, whole step, whole step, whole step, half step.

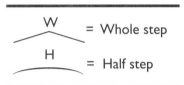

C Major Scale

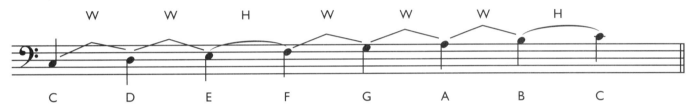

The major scale consists of seven different notes, one for each letter of the musical alphabet. The scale gets its name from the first note, or *tonic*, of the scale. You may also hear the tonic referred to as the *root* of the scale. In the case below, because we are going from C to C, the scale is a C Major scale.

The octave, or 8th note in the scale, allows us to divide the scale into two groups of four notes. These groupings of four consecutive notes are *tetrachords*. Below, you can see that the major scale is made of two tetrachords that share the same pattern of whole steps and half steps: W–W–H. The tetrachords are separated by one whole step.

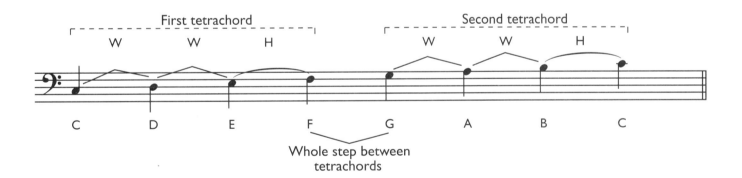

Thinking about the major scale in terms of tetrachords will make it easier for you to figure out various fingerings across the fretboard of the bass. Being able to play the major scale in more than one way will give you greater versatility as a bassist and will make your playing much more fun.

Applying the Major Scale to the Fretboard

The diagram below shows a basic fingering for the C Major scale starting on the 3rd fret of the 3rd string. The numbers next to the circles indicate which left-hand finger to use for that fretted note. Notice that the first and last notes of the scale are indicated by a hollow dot (○); this is to show the tonic or root note of the scale. The two tetrachords that make up this fingering are highlighted.

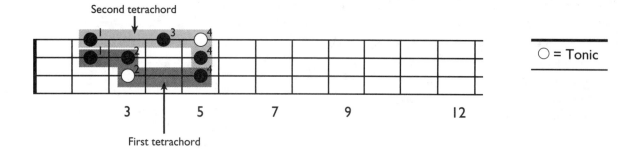

○ = Tonic

Use the fingering above to play the following exercise. This will get you familiar with the sound and feel of the major scale. Play the exercise many times, starting slowly, and as you get a better handle on the scale, you can pick up the tempo. Again, be sure to alternate your right-hand picking fingers for each note.

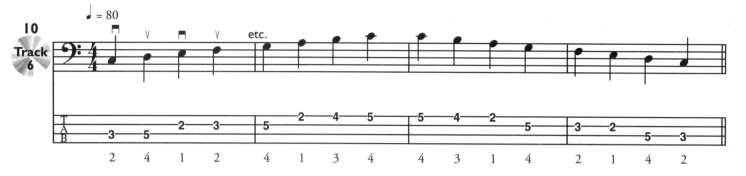

This next fingering for the C Major Scale is played on only two strings, and has two shifts of hand position. The shifts occur between the 1st and 2nd notes (C and D) and the 5th and 6th notes (G and A) of the scale. With this fingering, it is very easy to visualize the two tetrachords that make up the major scale.

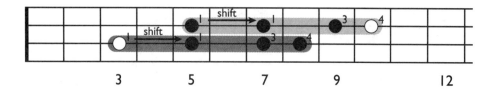

Again, play the C Major scale pattern up and down, using the fingering above. To get to know the note names all over the fretboard, say the name of each note as you play it.

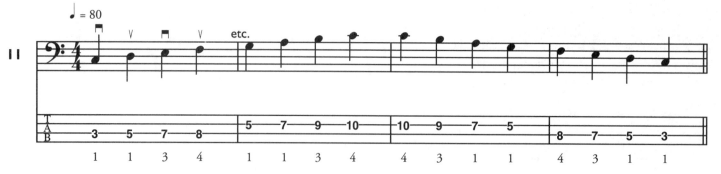

It is also useful to be able to play the entire major scale across one string. This example uses the E Major scale, which is made up of the notes: E–F♯–G♯–A–B–C♯–D♯.

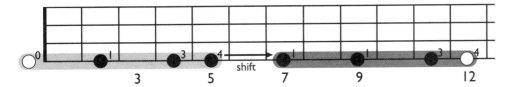

Notice that this scale has accidentals (F♯, G♯, C♯, and D♯). To play any major scale, we must follow the formula of whole steps and half steps, no matter what pitch we start on. So, in order to build a major scale starting on E, we need to use these sharps. We can't use flats, because each pitch in the scale needs its own letter name, in alphabetical order. If flats were used instead of sharps, the scale would be spelled E–G♭–A♭–A–B–D♭–E♭–E, which does not fit into that rule.

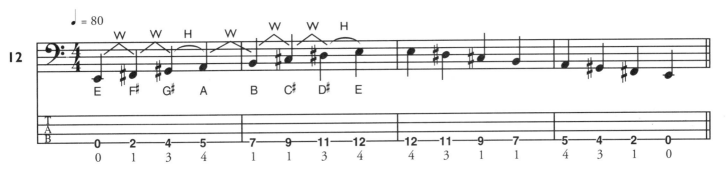

Scale Degrees

Another helpful tool in understanding scale construction and music theory is the use of *scale degrees*. This is a simple concept where numbers are assigned to each note of the major scale: 1 through 7.

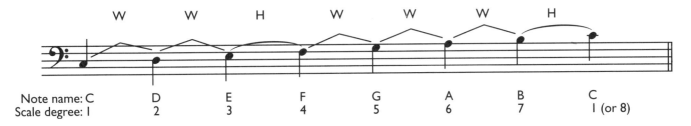

Remember, there are two occurrences of half steps in the major scale: between scale degrees 3 and 4, and 7 and 8. Scale degrees 8 and 1 are interchangeable, because 8 is an octave above 1 and has the same note name.

If you think about the major scale construction using scale degrees, and use the concept of tetrachords to visualize fingerings on the fretboard, you will be able to easily create the major scale starting on any note. The fingerings shown so far are not the only fingerings for the major scale. Take some time to use the major scale formula to figure out additional fingerings for this scale.

Major Scale Exercises

These exercises are designed to do three things:

1. Develop your reading skills

2. Increase finger strength and ability to stretch

3. Reinforce the feel and sound of the major scale

Although these exercises may not sound much like rock music, they are meant simply to build up your abilities. By using these exercises to increase strength and reinforce musical knowledge, you will be able to more easily apply rock techniques and "feel" to your bass lines.

The following exercise uses a consistent rhythm of quarter notes, as well as the first fingering of the C Major scale. Practice this slowly, and you will gradually build more strength and be able to play it faster and faster. Pay close attention to the fingerings.

This next exercise features the major scale played entirely on one string; in this case, the 1st string. Be sure to notice the F#s that occur in the G Major scale. Because this pattern moves up the neck to the 12th fret, it will get you used to traversing the fretboard. Again, pay attention to the fingerings below the TAB and note any changes or shifts in hand position.

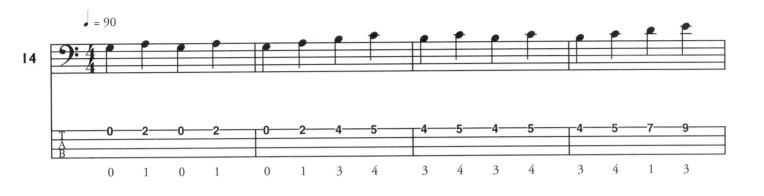

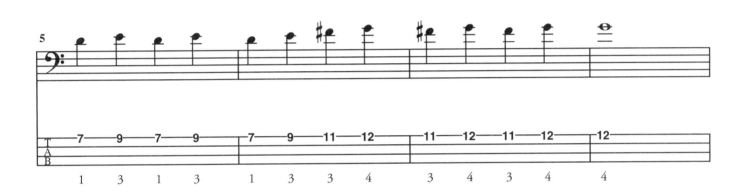

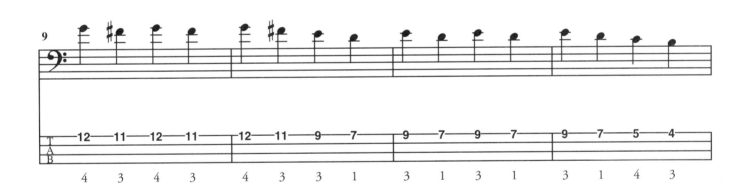

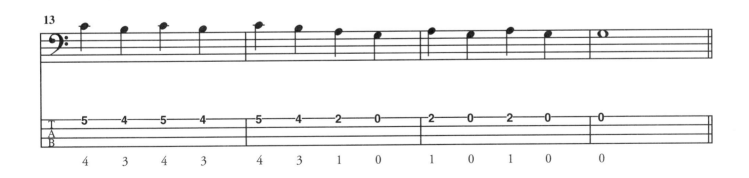

Intervals

In music, an *interval* is the distance in pitch between any two notes. Each interval has a specific name related to the distance between the two notes. In the major scale, every interval from the tonic will be called either a *major* or a *perfect* interval.

For example, the distance between the root and the 2nd note of the major scale is called a major 2nd, and the distance between the root and the 3rd note of the major scale is called a major 3rd. The only perfect intervals are between the root and the 4th, the root and the 5th, and the root and the octave.

If you lower a major interval by a half step, it becomes a *minor* interval. If you lower perfect interval by a half step, it becomes a *diminished* interval. And if you raise a perfect interval by a half step, it becomes an *augmented* interval.

The Intervals

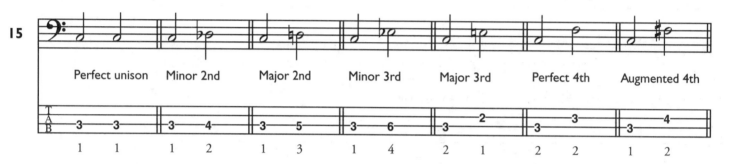

Practice playing and saying the names of these intervals aloud. A good idea is to find the different fingering choices for each one, and then associate that fingering with the name of that interval.

For instance, to play a minor 2nd, you play the note that is one fret higher than the tonic. So you know that when you move up by just one fret, you are playing an interval of a minor 2nd.

For now, simply play each interval and say the interval name aloud several times. You'll notice that the augmented 4th and the diminished 5th intervals sound the same; this is because they are enharmonic equivalents. This interval can also simply be called the *tritone* because it consists of three whole steps.

Key Signatures

Remember, whenever the tonic of our major scale is any note other than C, we need to use accidentals to maintain the formula of whole steps and half steps (see page 23).

When we play a piece with all or most of the notes based in one scale, we say we are playing in that *key*. For instance, if you play a piece using only notes in the C Major scale, you can say you are playing in the key of C Major. At the beginning of most pieces is a *key signature*, which shows the notes that are to be played either sharp or flat throughout the piece. This useful device makes the music easier to read, because it reduces the number of accidentals that have to be written.

The following example shows the A Major scale written using accidentals.

The example below shows the A Major scale written using the key signature of A Major. Notice the key signature has sharp signs on the lines and spaces for each note that previously had an accidental: F♯, C♯, and G♯. Even though the actual notes do not have sharp signs next to them, the key signature tells us to always play these notes sharp (unless told otherwise by a different accidental).

Key signature   C♯   F♯   G♯

The Circle of 5ths

The *circle of 5ths* is a tool that represents every possible key signature and how they are related. Going around in a clockwise direction, you can see that each key is a perfect 5th away from the previous key. (At the moment, we are only concerned with the major keys: C, G, D, etc. However, for each major key, there is a relative minor key that shares the same key signature. For more on this, see page 71.)

As the key signatures progress, one sharp is added. Once you reach the key of B, which has five sharps, the enharmonic key of C♭ has seven flats. If you keep proceeding in a clockwise motion, you then subtract flats from the key signatures. Another way to look at the flat keys is to progress in a counterclockwise direction from the key of C. Each new key is a perfect 5th down from the previous key (for example, count five down from C and you get F: **C**–B–A–G–**F**). As the key signatures progress in this direction, one flat is added.

You will never see a key signature with both sharps and flats; it's one or the other. Notice that the only key with no sharps or flats is the key of C Major.

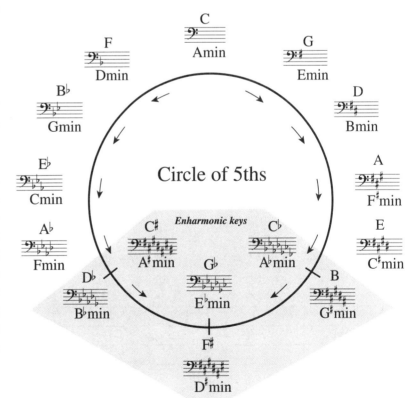

Figuring Out Key Signatures

A simple way to memorize the correct order of sharps is with the saying "Father Charles Goes Down And Ends Battle" (F♯, C♯, G♯, D♯, A♯, E♯, B♯). To remember the correct order of flats, you simply reverse the saying to "Battle Ends And Down Goes Charles Father" (B♭, E♭, A♭, D♭, G♭, C♭, F♭).

If you have trouble memorizing the circle of 5ths, or identifying key signatures, there are two simple methods for figuring out keys based on key signatures:

1. **Sharp key signatures.** The method for key signatures with sharps in them is to simply go up one half step from the last sharp listed. For example, if you see four sharps in the key signature (F♯, C♯, G♯, D♯), you go one half step up from D♯ and get E, so you know you are in the key of E Major.

E Major

One half step up from D♯ is E

2. **Flat key signatures.** To figure out the key of a flat key signature, you simply name it after the second to last flat listed. For example, if you see four flats in the key signature (B♭, E♭, A♭, D♭), the second to last flat is A♭, so you know you are in the key of A♭.

A♭ Major

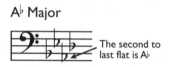

The second to last flat is A♭

Two-Octave Major Scale Fingerings

Now that you are familiar with the feel and sound of the major scale, as well as the theory behind it, you can get comfortable playing it over the entire neck. The following two-octave major scale fingerings will take you all over the neck and provide more options for building your own bass lines. These are not the only two-octave major scale fingerings; take some time and figure out others on your own.

Practice playing them up and down, and again, try creating your own patterns and exercises.

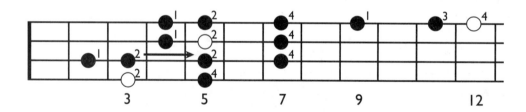

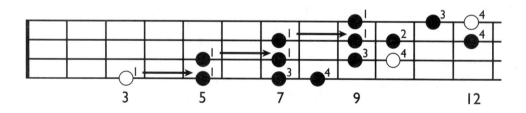

Major Scale Bass Lines

The following bass lines have been created using notes from the major scale. Pay attention to the key signature, and note that each exercise will use the different fingerings we have covered.

This first bass line uses our first fingering and requires no shifting of hand position. Notice the double barline at the end with the two dots. This is called a *repeat sign* and tells you to go back to the beginning and play it again without stopping. Also, notice the key signature of G Major (one sharp).

Repeat sign

The second bass line uses the shifting major scale pattern across two strings; it is in F Major (one flat).

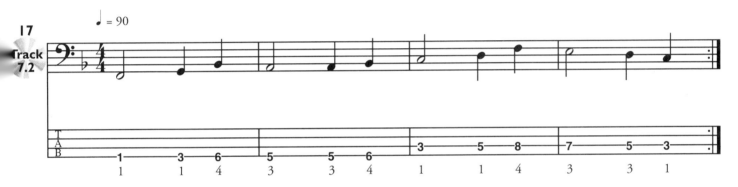

This third bass line is in the key of A Major (three sharps). It covers two octaves and uses open strings.

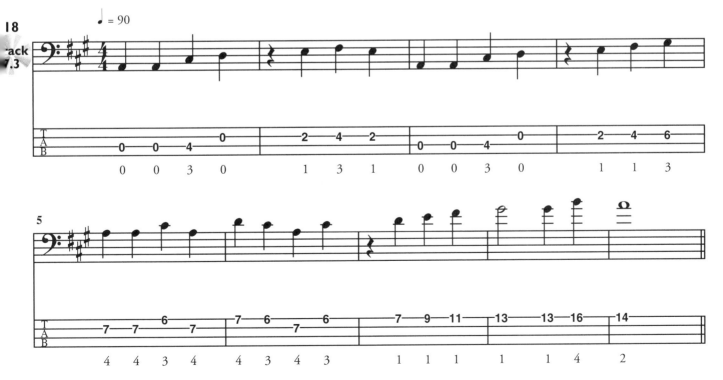

Rhythm Practice: Eighth Notes

Just as whole notes were broken down into half notes, and half notes into quarter notes, quarter notes can be broken down into eighth notes. An eighth note gets one half of a beat in $\frac{4}{4}$ time. You will see these notes written either with flags, or beamed together in groups of two or four. Just like any other note value, the eighth note has its corresponding rest.

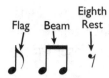

The common practice for counting note values that are smaller than one beat is to *subdivide*. This means that we break the beat into smaller parts. For eighth notes, instead of counting "1, 2, 3, 4," we divide the beat in half and count "1 and, 2 and, 3 and, 4 and." When this is written out, an ampersand "&" is used to represent the "ands" of the beat. Counting in this manner is very important, especially when you are playing bass lines that incorporate a lot of complex rhythms.

If you were to tap your foot to the beat of a song in $\frac{4}{4}$ time, each time your foot came up would be the "and" of the beat, also known as the *offbeat*. (The *onbeats* are represented by the numbers themselves: 1, 2, 3, 4.)

The following exercise can be seen as a "bass aerobics" workout designed to get your right hand in shape, and also to get you used to playing eighth notes. Be sure to start slowly and count aloud. As you master this exercise at one tempo, increase the speed and practice it at faster tempos. Using a metronome when playing this exercise will really help you improve your right-hand abilities. Be sure to alternate between your 1st and 2nd right-hand fingers, or upstrokes and downstrokes of the pick, in order to get the most out of this exercise. Developing good alternate picking will allow you to play at faster tempos much more easily.

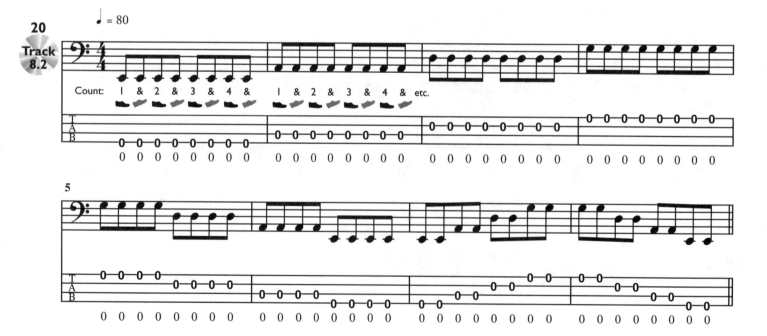

Eighth-Note Exercises

The following exercise will get you familiar with using eighth notes and other note values. Here, it is especially helpful to subdivide when counting.

21
Track
9.1

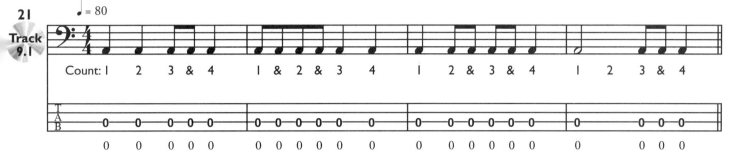

Eighth rests are often used to create *syncopation*. Syncopation occurs when emphasis is placed on the offbeats. It is very important to count aloud and subdivide when reading bass lines with eighth rests. Again, be sure to properly mute the strings when playing the rests. Note that counting numbers for rests are in parentheses.

22
Track
9.2

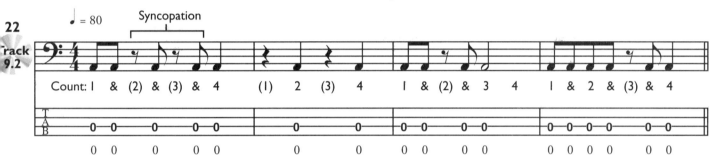

The following rhythmic exercise uses even greater syncopation. Note that the first note is actually a rest, so you come in on the "and" of beat 1. Be sure to take this one slowly at first, and as always, be sure to count.

23
Track
9.3

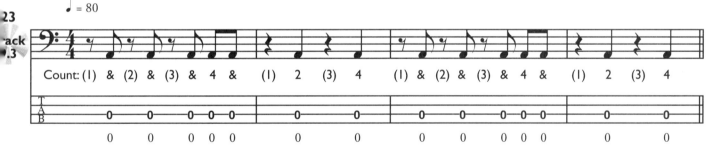

This exercise uses every note value and rest value that has been covered so far. Be sure to read ahead and prepare to subdivide your counting when playing eighth notes. Also, be extra patient when counting whole notes or whole rests after playing a string of eighth notes. There can be a tendency to want to rush through them after playing quickly.

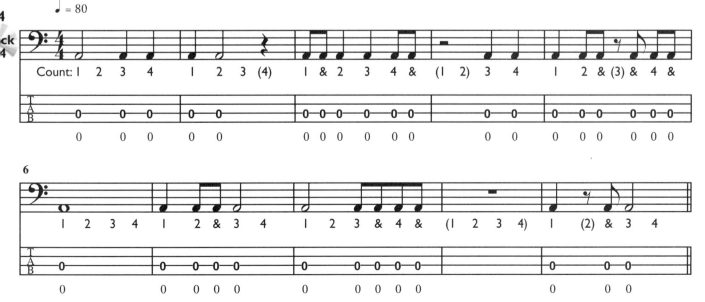

Ties

There are other ways of altering note values, and one of them is using *ties*. Ties link notes of the same pitch together and combine their values. A tie is a curved line that goes from one notehead to another. The example below shows two quarter notes tied together. Because the tie combines their value, these tied notes get a total of two beats. So, you only play the note for the first quarter note, but let it ring through the second note. Ties can only be used on notes of the same pitch.

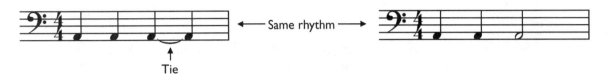

Tie

So far, the note values discussed cover only four beats, two beats, one beat, or half of a beat. Now, by using ties, we can have note values of three beats, one and a half beats, or two and a half beats.

3 beats   1½ beats   2½ beats

Ties also allow us to create more intricate rhythms by allowing us to tie notes together across barlines. Even though a note value is tied across a barline, you would still count the first beat of the measure as "1," but not play again until beat 2.

Count: 1   2   3   4   1   2   3   4

The following example uses only quarter-note and half-note rhythms with ties. Be sure to keep your counting accurate, and let the tied notes ring for their correct values.

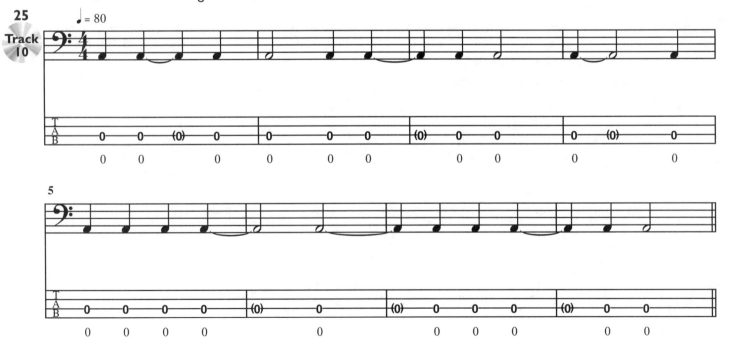

Hammer-Ons and Pull-Offs

Hammer-ons and *pull-offs* are techniques used to create smoother, connected, more fluid sounds. This is known as playing *legato*.

To play a hammer-on using open strings, pluck the open string, and then press down any finger of your left hand on any fret. You can apply the same technique between fretted notes as well. You must make sure to press hard enough that the second note sounds, but also make sure to not play the second note using your right hand.

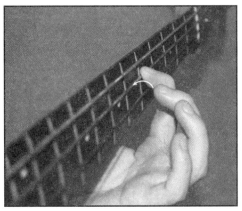

Preparing for hammer-on.

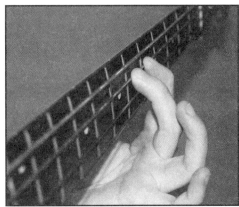

Completion of hammer-on.

Playing pull-offs is the reverse of playing hammer-ons. Play the fretted note, and then pull the string using your left-hand finger to get the second fretted or open note to sound. You cannot just lift the finger up off of the fretboard. If you are playing a pull-off between two fretted notes, you must make sure that both left hand fingers are on the fretboard before playing the pull-off.

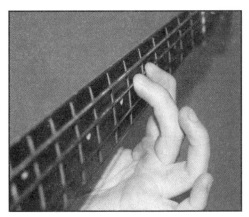

Preparing for pull-off.

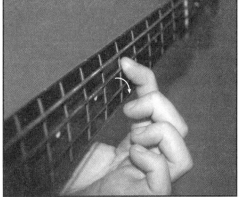

Completion of pull-off.

Legato techniques such as hammer-ons and pull-offs are indicated with *slurs*. Slurs look identical to ties, however, they connect two notes of different pitches, whereas ties connect notes of the same pitch. In the TAB, you will see an H above the slur to indicate a hammer-on, while a PO above the slur indicates a pull-off.

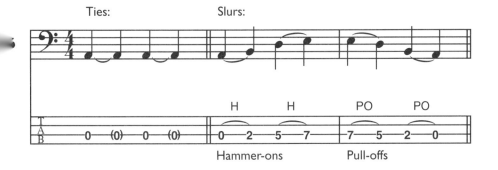

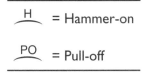

H = Hammer-on

PO = Pull-off

Legato Exercises

These exercises are designed to build left-hand finger strength for playing hammer-ons and pull-offs.

This exercise focuses on playing open-string hammer-ons using each finger. Be sure to play this exercise across all strings.

This next exercise is similar, only you will play pull-offs and start from the 1st string using your 4th finger. Be aware of how hard you need to pull to get the note to sound. You want to avoid accidentally hitting any adjacent strings.

When you are comfortable with both of these exercises, try combining them by ascending using hammer-ons and descending using pull-offs.

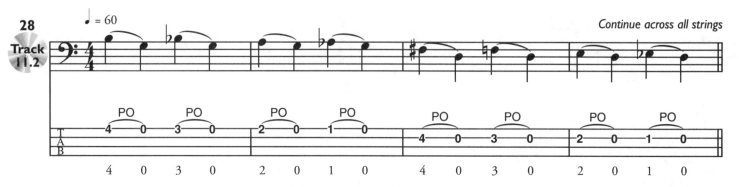

The following exercise will play up and down the major scale using hammer-ons and pull-offs. Make sure that when pulling off from one fretted note to another, you have the left-hand finger for the second note already in position.

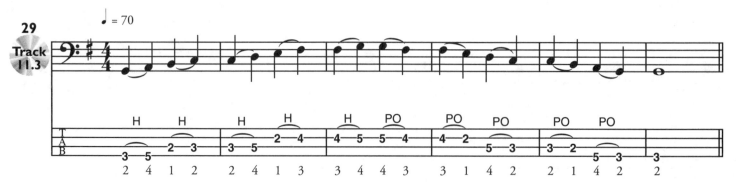

Simple Rock Bass Lines

The following bass lines will combine almost everything that has been covered so far.

This first bass line is in the style of "Love Me Do" by the Beatles. Although it's played with mainly a half-note rhythm, try and keep the feel upbeat and quick.

This next bass line is in the style of the chorus to "Bound for the Floor" by Local H. Although it uses all the same notes as the C Major scale, it is actually in the *relative*

minor key of A Minor (for more on this, see page 71). To get the feel of the rhythm, be sure to nail those ties.

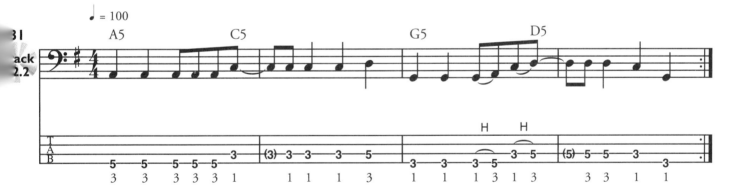

This next simple bass line is in the style of "Float On" by Modest Mouse. It uses a simple, but effective, rhythm that locks in with the drums.

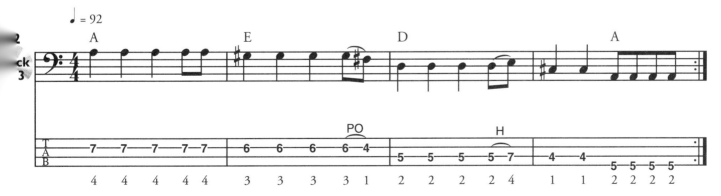

Chapter 4: Intro to Harmony

The role of a bass player is not only to provide extra low end to what a guitarist or keyboard player may already be playing, but also to provide *harmony*. Harmony is the act of combining simultaneous pitches into chords. Most often, the way bassists create harmony is to outline chords or emphasize certain parts of chords within the music. Being able to outline chords and recognize chord progressions is a skill that all bass players must have. It's very common for beginning rock bassists to simply play the root note of the chord, or to double what the guitar player is playing for a riff or a hook; however, outlining the harmony and playing something different can create thicker textures within the music.

Intervals

As discussed earlier (page 28), an interval is the distance between any two notes. There are two types of intervals used in music: *melodic intervals* and *harmonic intervals*. Melodic intervals refer to two notes being played in succession, whereas harmonic intervals refer to two notes being played at the same time. Most of the time, bass players will be using melodic intervals. This section will outline different non-shifting fingerings for each interval and provide ways to recognize that interval when hearing it by using familiar tunes or songs.

Minor 2nd
Distance: One half step (ex. C to D♭)
Sounds like: Theme from the movie *Jaws*

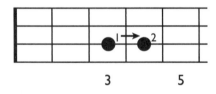

Major 2nd
Distance: One whole step, or two half steps (ex. C to D)
Sounds like: "You Really Got Me" by the Kinks

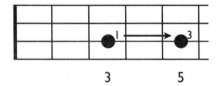
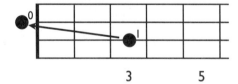

Minor 3rd
Distance: One-and-a-half whole steps, or three half steps (ex. C to E♭)
Sounds like: First two notes of "Hey Man Nice Shot" by Filter

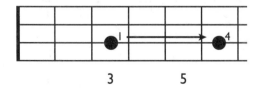
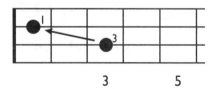

Major 3rd

Distance: Two whole steps, or four half steps (ex. C to E)
Sounds like: First two notes of "Blister in the Sun" by the Violent Femmes

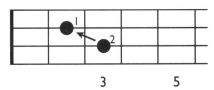 

Perfect 4th

Distance: Two-and-a-half whole steps, or five half steps (ex. C to F)
Sounds like: First two chords of "Smells like Teen Spirit" by Nirvana, or Wagner's "Bridal Chorus" (a.k.a. "Here Comes the Bride")

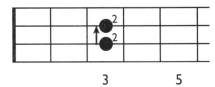 

Augmented 4th/Diminished 5th/Tritone

Distance: Three whole steps, or six half steps (ex. C to F♯, or C to G♭)
Sounds like: First two notes of the theme from "The Simpsons," or the introductory riff to "YYZ" by Rush

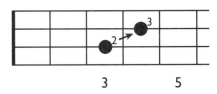 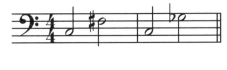

Perfect 5th

Distance: Three-and-a-half whole steps, or seven half steps (ex. C to G)
Sounds like: First two chords of "When I Come Around" by Green Day

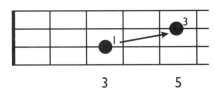 

Minor 6th

Distance: Four whole steps, or eight half steps (ex. C to A♭)
Sounds like: First two chords of "Self Esteem" by the Offspring

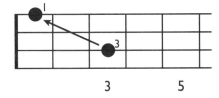 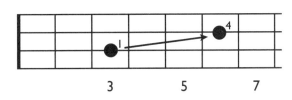 

Major 6th

Distance: Four-and-a-half whole steps, or nine half steps (ex. C to A)
Sounds like: First two notes of the NBC Theme

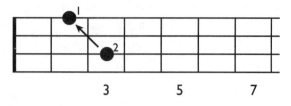 

Minor 7th

Distance: Five whole steps, or ten half steps (ex. C to B♭)
Sounds like: First two chords of "Back in Black" by AC/DC

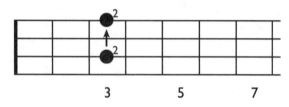 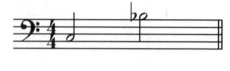

Major 7th

Distance: Five-and-a-half whole steps, or eleven half steps (ex. C to B)
Sounds like: The opening guitar riff to "Popular" by Nada Surf

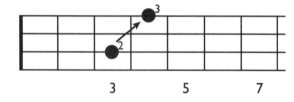 

Perfect Octave

Distance: Six whole steps, or twelve half steps (ex. C to C)
Sounds like: First two notes of "Tom Sawyer" by Rush, or first two notes of "Over the Rainbow"

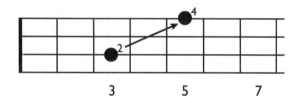 

Interval Inversions

When we play a melodic interval in reverse, we are *inverting* the interval, or playing its *inversion*. For example, a perfect 5th is played from C up to G, but to invert it would be to play from G up to C, or from C down to G, and those would both now be perfect 4ths.

The rules for inverting intervals is that both the interval and its inversion add up to nine (5th plus 4th or 5 + 4 = 9). When inverting intervals, the inversion has the opposite harmonic quality. For example, a major 3rd inverts to become a minor 6th, a minor 2nd inverts to a major 7th, and an augmented 4th inverts to a diminished 5th. Perfect intervals remain perfect.

Note name: C   G   G   C   C   G

Triads

In order to outline chords and create harmony in our bass lines, we need to understand just what makes up a chord. The most basic type of chord is called a *triad* and consists of three notes. The term "triad" refers to the fact they have only three notes, which are separated from each other by the interval of a 3rd. Like intervals, each triad has a harmonic quality of major, minor, diminished, or augmented.

Each triad is built of a root, the 3rd above that root, and a 5th above the root. The root note gives the triad its letter name, while the 3rd determines the harmonic quality of the triad: major or minor. The following fingerings are only basic fingerings for each triad. See what other fingerings you can figure out on your own using the triad formula.

Major Triads

To create a C Major triad, we have a root (C), a major 3rd above that (E), and a perfect 5th above the root (G).

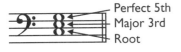

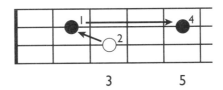

Minor Triads

The C Minor triad consists of a root (C), minor 3rd (E♭), and a perfect 5th (G).

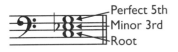

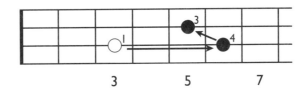

Diminished Triads

The C Diminished triad consists of a root (C), minor 3rd (E♭) and a diminished 5th (G♭). Notice that this triad is made of stacked minor 3rds, and that its harmonic quality comes from the diminished 5th with the minor 3rd.

 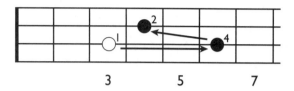

Augmented Triads

The C Augmented triad consists of the root (C), major 3rd (E), and augmented 5th (G♯). This triad is made of stacked major 3rds and is much rarer than the others.

 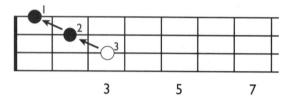

Reading Chord Symbols

Chord symbols are commonly written above the staff to show just what chords are being played or implied. The chord symbols show the name and harmonic quality of each chord. Shown to the right are the different options for writing chord symbols (using C as the root). Once you become familiar with the common triad shapes and sounds, you will be able to read chord charts made up only of chord symbols and spontaneously write bass lines that accurately outline each chord.

Chord	Chord Symbol
C Major	C or C△
C Minor	Cmin or C-
C Diminished	Cdim or C°
C Augmented	Caug or C+

The process of playing chords one note at a time is known as playing *arpeggios*, which are sometimes called "broken chords." The following exercise will have you arpeggiate all four triad shapes. Note the chord symbols above the staff. Once you have completed this exercise, play these triad shapes on different roots all over the neck.

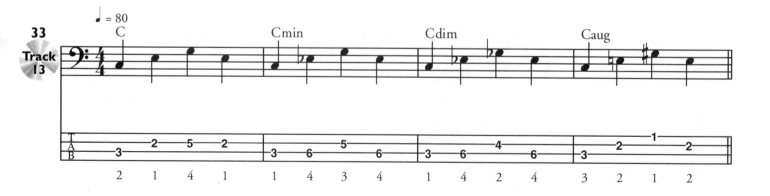

This exercise shows the triad shapes with their roots on the open strings.

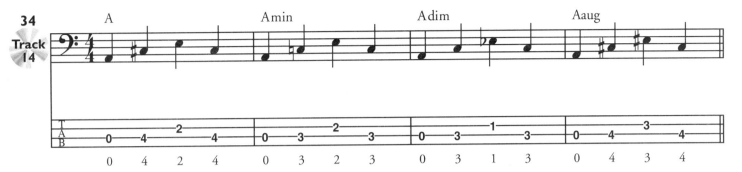

The following staff shows only the chord symbols and no standard music notation or TAB. This is written in the style of a *lead sheet*. Lead sheets outline the harmony of the song to be played, and it is up to the performer to decide how to play each chord. *Slash notation* indicates how many beats are in each measure using a slash symbol ╱, but it does not dictate that you play any particular rhythm or bass line. Try applying your triad fingerings while reading these chord names. You can practice along with the backing track on the CD as well.

Diatonic Harmony

The term *diatonic* basically means "within the key." So, if we say we are playing notes that are diatonic to the key of C Major, then we know we are playing notes within the key of C Major. When we talk about *diatonic harmony*, we are referring to all the chords that occur naturally within a key.

If you build triads on each scale degree of the major scale, you will get the diatonic harmony for a major key. The example below shows the triads built in the key of C Major as well as their name and qualities. Just as you memorized the pattern of whole steps and half steps for the major scale, it's a good idea to memorize the order of the harmonic qualities of the major scale: major–minor–minor–major–major–minor–diminished–major (see example below).

With the major scale, we assigned each note a scale degree, and we will do the same with chords. However, because chords each have a different harmonic quality, we cannot use ordinary numerals like 1, 2, 3, etc. In order to indicate the scale degree on which these chords occur and also their harmonic qualities, Roman numerals are used. An upper-case Roman numeral means that the chord is major, and a lower-case Roman numeral means the chord is minor. Diminished chords are lower case with the ° symbol, and augmented chords are upper case with the + symbol.

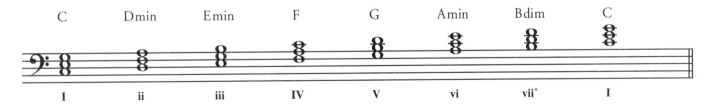

Notice above that only three chords are major in quality: the I, IV, and the V. These three chords are known as the *primary chords* of the key. A ton of rock tunes are made using mostly (or only) the primary chords. A couple of examples are "Blitzkrieg Bop" by the Ramones and "I Fought the Law" as performed by the Clash. (For more on the I–IV–V progression, see page 60.)

The chart below shows each triad and exactly how it is spelled in the key of C Major. You should become very familiar with these spellings, because they will help you to better understand and analyze chords from other keys in the future.

Triad Name	Roman Numeral	Triad Spelling
C Major	I	C–E–G
D Minor	ii	D–F–A
E Minor	iii	E–G–B
F Major	IV	F–A–C
G Major	V	G–B–D
A Minor	vi	A–C–E
B Diminished	vii°	B–D–F

Triad Exercises

The next couple of exercises will have you arpeggiating through each diatonic chord in different keys. Pay attention not only to the fingerings, but to the chord symbols as well. Once you have mastered this exercise, try reading just the chord symbols, and try using different fingerings.

This first exercise is in the key of C Major and uses the basic triad shapes moving up the neck, keeping the triad roots on the 3rd string.

This next exercise is in the key of G and moves across all four strings. This exercise requires no position-shifting of the left hand, but will use some different fingerings for certain triads.

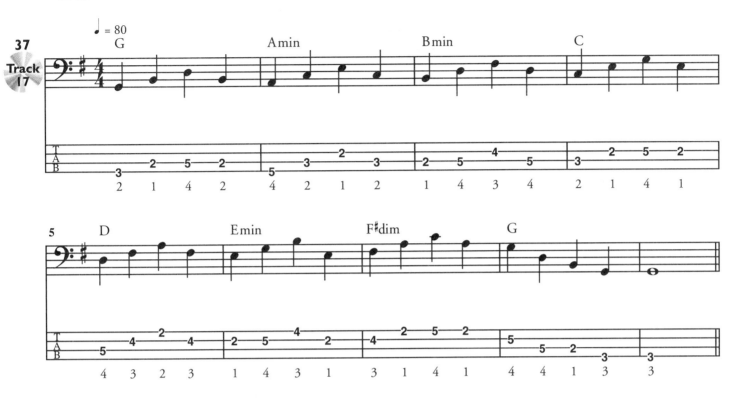

Rhythm Practice: Dotted Notes

Ties are not the only way we can increase the rhythmic value of a note. Another method is the use of *dotted* notes. The simple act of adding a dot after a note increases that note's rhythmic value by one half of the original note value.

For instance, if you have a half note (two beats) and add a dot after it, the new value is three beats. The same concept applies to rests as well.

$$\textrm{♩} + \cdot = \textrm{♩·} \qquad \textbf{—} + \cdot = \textbf{—·}$$
$$2 + 1 = 3 \qquad\qquad 2 + 1 = 3$$

Practice reading and playing dotted half-note rhythms in the following exercise.

If you add a dot after a quarter note, the new note value is the original value (1), plus half of that (½), which would equal one-and-a-half beats.

Often, you will see a dotted quarter note followed by an eighth note or an eighth rest.

Any note following a dotted quarter note will be played on the offbeat. So be sure to keep your counting consistent if you see a dotted quarter note followed by a quarter note, a half note, or another dotted quarter note. These rhythms are tricky and are good examples of syncopation.

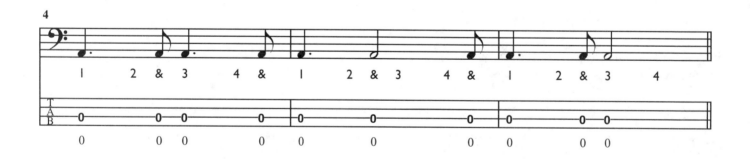

Bass Lines Using Triads

The following bass lines use many of the triad shapes covered so far. Pay attention to the fingerings, as well as the chord symbols.

The following is a typical ska bass line. The eighth-note rhythm pushes it forward, while the notes of the triads outline the chords of the song.

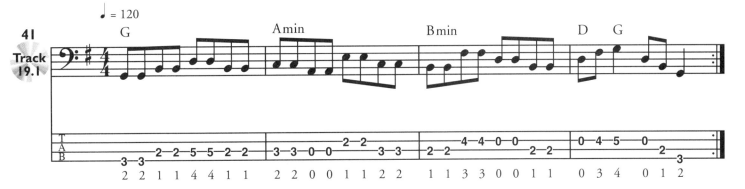

The next bass line follows a common pop-punk chord progression using hammer-ons, pull-offs, and dotted quarter rhythms.

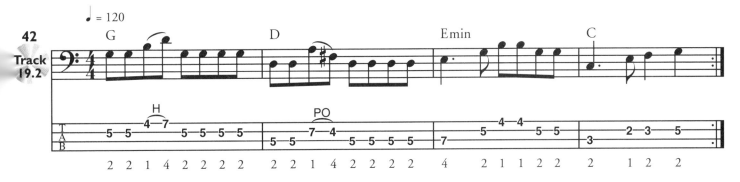

In the bass line below, dotted quarter-note rhythms are used to create a reggae-style groove.

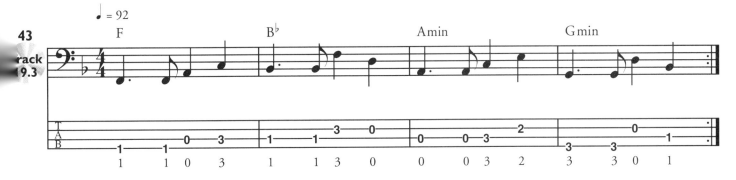

This next bass line is based on a classical bass pattern known as *Alberti bass*. The pattern consists of the root, 5th, 3rd, and 5th of each chord played in sequence. Sometimes, applying different musical styles to a rock context can create original sounds. The bass line below moves across the 4th and 3rd strings, with the root of each chord on the 4th string. This requires you to shift your hand position for each chord.

Chapter 5: Expanding Harmony—7th Chords

Harmony is not limited to the use of triads. In this section, we'll discuss four-note chords known as *7th chords*. These chords are built by adding either a major 7th or minor 7th above the root of a triad. This creates more harmonic possibilities, and understanding these chords will help you to create effective bass lines.

Similar to the interval of a 3rd, 7ths can either be major or minor, which means there is a greater variety of 7th chords to learn. However, some are less common than others. The following three are the most common.

Major 7th Chords

The *major 7* chord consists of a major triad with a major 7th above the root, which you can easily remember as being a half step below the octave.

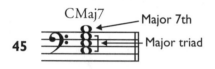
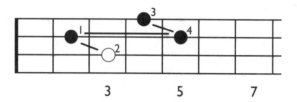

Minor 7th Chords

The *minor 7* chord consists of a minor triad with a minor 7th above the root, which can easily be remembered as being a whole step below the octave.

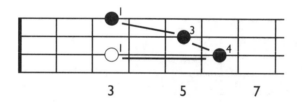

Dominant 7th Chords

Next is the *dominant 7* chord, which consists of a major triad with a minor 7th above the root. Note that its symbol is just the letter name followed by a 7.

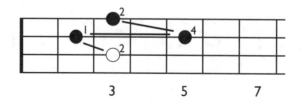

These next 7th chords are not found as often in rock music but are useful in certain situations.

Half-Diminished 7th Chord

The *half-diminished 7th* chord consists of a diminished triad with a minor 7th above the root. This chord is also known as the minor $7^\flat5$. You may see the symbol written as a min$7^\flat5$ or as the diminished symbol with a slash through it $^\varnothing$.

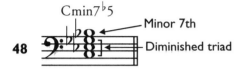

48

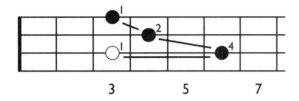

Diminished 7th Chord

The *diminished 7th* chord consists of a diminished triad with a diminished 7th above the root. It is important to note that just as the diminished triad was built of stacked minor 3rds, the diminished 7th chord is also built of all stacked minor 3rds. Also, notice that the diminished 7th is a half step below the minor 7th. Because the 7th has to be a form of B in the key of C, in this case it is B double-flat (B$^{\flat\flat}$). It is enharmonic to A natural.

$\flat\flat$ = *Double flat.* Lowers the pitch of a note by two half steps.

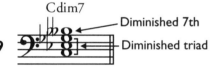

49

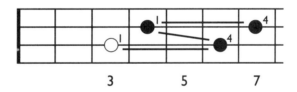

Minor-Major 7th Chord

The *minor-major 7th* chord consists of a minor triad with a major 7th on top. It is notated with the symbol minMaj7.

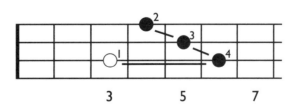

Diatonic 7th Chords

Just as with triads, if we build our 7th chords using only notes from the major scale stacked on top of each scale degree, we get the 7th chords that are diatonic to the major key. Notice that the V chord, G7, is the only dominant 7th chord, and that the vii chord, Bmin7♭5, is the only half-diminished chord.

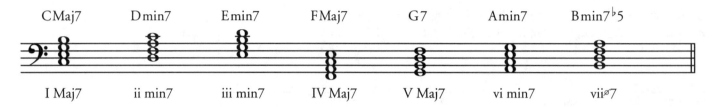

The following exercise has you arpeggiate through each diatonic 7th chord in the key of C Major, with each root located on the 3rd string.

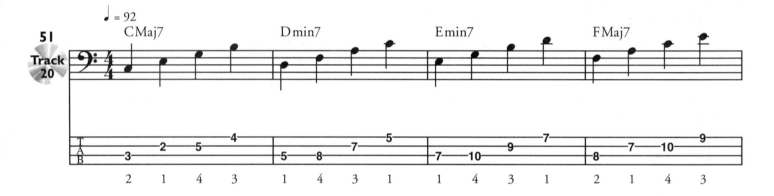

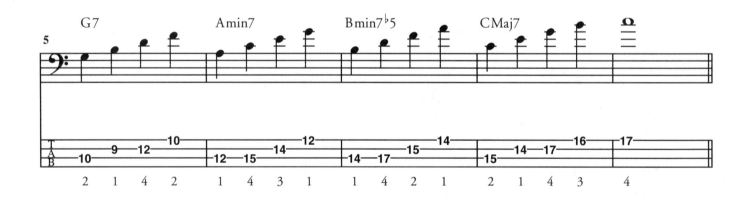

This exercise is in the key of G Major and arpeggiates through each 7th chord, staying mostly in one position, but shifting once we reach the vi chord.

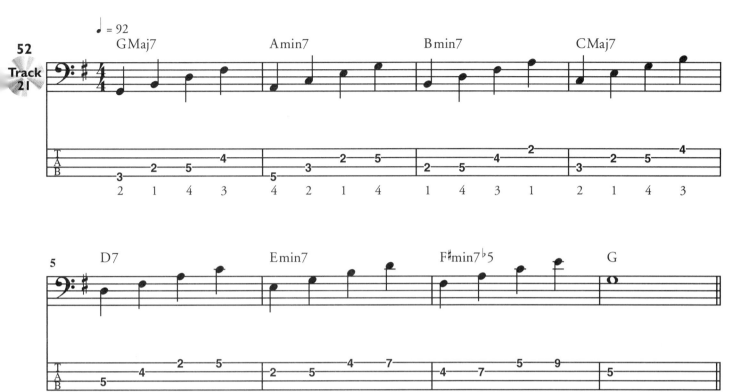

With rock bass lines, we don't always have to outline the 7th chords by playing every note within them. In rock music, we see dominant 7th chords more often than any other kind of 7th chord, and it is important to outline the ♭7 of this chord to really emphasize its flavor.

As we saw when looking at the diatonic 7th chord harmony of the major scale, the V chord is our only diatonic dominant 7. We almost always see V chords as V7 chords. By targeting the ♭7th of that chord, we really emphasize the *resolution* back to the I chord by creating more tension. So in most rock music, if you see a dominant 7th chord, you can generally assume that it is being used as the V chord. However, there are exceptions to this, especially in blues, blues rock, and progressive rock.

Rhythm Practice: Sixteenth Notes

To play blistering fast bass lines, we need to break down our rhythmic values yet again. Just as the quarter note divides in half to get two eighth notes, eighth notes divide into two halves to get *sixteenth notes*. So, two sixteenth notes equal one eighth note, which means there are four sixteenth notes per quarter note, or beat.

Sixteenth rest

Now, just as we subdivided the beat into "1 and, 2 and, 3 and, 4 and" with eighth notes, we need to further subdivide our counting with sixteenth notes. To count sixteenth notes, we use "1–e–&–a" (one–ee–and–uh).

Track 22.1

Count: 1 e & a 2 e & a 3 e & a 4 e & a

Following is another bass aerobic workout to get you used to playing sixteenth notes across each string. When playing sixteenth notes, be sure to keep your right-hand fingers alternating, or if you are using a pick, use your alternate-picking technique.

53
Track 22.2

♩ = 72

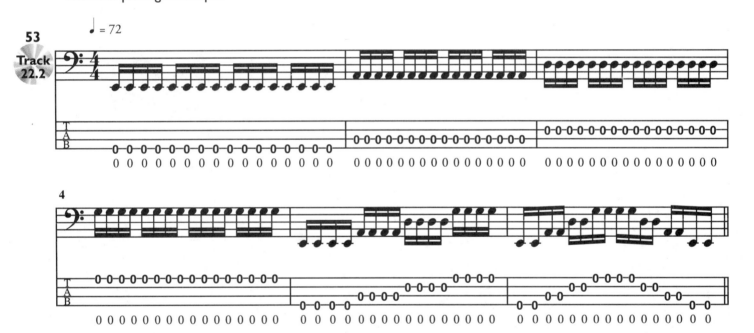

Just as we saw that dotted quarter notes are often followed by eighth notes, dotted eighth notes are often followed by sixteenth notes. This is a very common rhythmic pattern that when repeated can generate almost a shuffle feel.

54
Track 22.3

♩ = 88

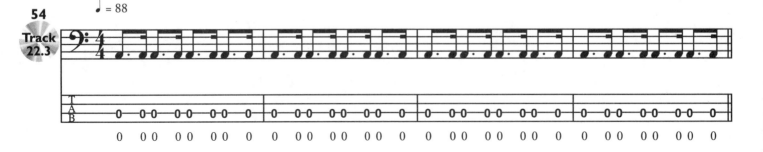

With the addition of sixteenth notes to our rhythmic choices, we can create a wide variety of rhythms within our bass lines. The following rhythmic exercises outline many common rhythmic patterns that use sixteenth notes.

This next exercise is a warm-up that will train both hands. It goes up the neck chromatically across all four strings, while also progressing rhythmically.

The following exercises are simple bass lines that utilize the occasional sixteenth-note rhythm.

This first one is in E Major and uses the non-shifting major scale fingering with the 2nd finger on the 7th fret of the 3rd string (another way to say this is that it's in 6th *position*, meaning your 1st finger is located at the 6th fret). As you play through the example, make sure to watch out for syncopated rhythms.

This next bass line has a darker sound, because it focuses on the minor chords of the key of C Major. It also employs a very popular rhythmic fill technique: the *two sixteenth/ eighth-note hammer-pull*. It is simply a hammer-on followed immediately by a pull-off to the same starting pitch.

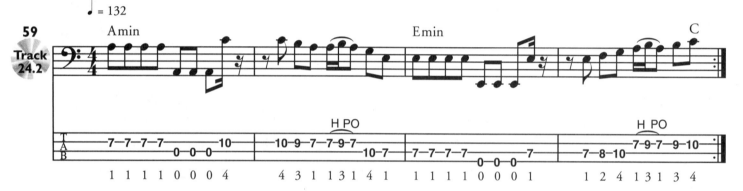

The bass line below is in the key of D Major and alternates between the iii and I chords using a "galloping" sixteenth-note rhythm. This rhythm has been used in countless heavy metal bass lines. Try working this rhythm up to be able to play it at very fast tempos. The bassist who is said to have pioneered this technique within the heavy metal genre is Iron Maiden's Steve Harris. Focus on keeping your right-hand fingers alternating.

This bass line has a disco-funk flavor to it.

Dead Notes

Dead notes are notes that are muted with the left hand to give a percussive sound to our bass lines. To play a dead note, you want to have the left-hand fingers touching the string, but not actually pressing it down to the fretboard because we don't want an actual pitch to sound.

This technique works great with sixteenth-note lines and is used a great deal in funk music. You may want to make sure that at least two of your left-hand fingers are touching the string. Dead notes are notated using X's.

$\times$ = Dead note

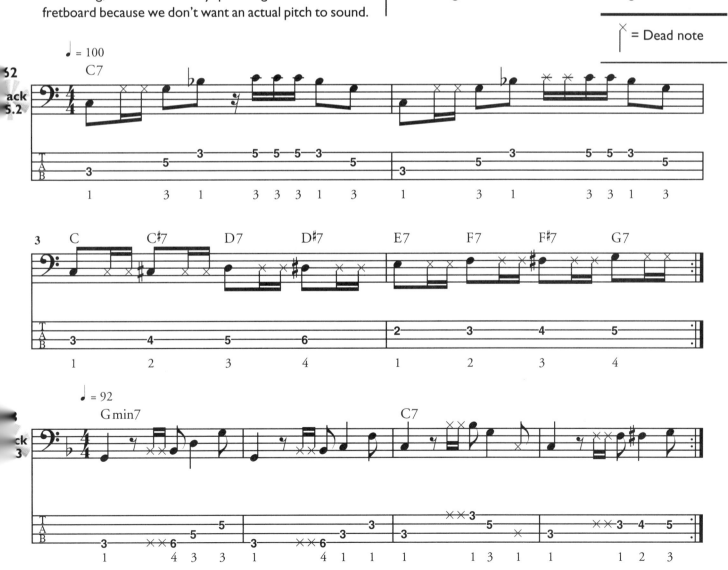

Slides

Another legato technique we can add alongside our hammer-ons and pull-offs is a technique we call *sliding*. Sliding involves moving our fingers along the fretboard from one note to another on the same string without lifting our fingers off the fretboard. We can use slides to help create smoother, more fluid melodic bass lines, or slippery, funky lines.

A slide is notated as a slur with a slanted line underneath it. If it is telling you to slide up the neck, the line will go from low to high; if it is telling you to slide downward, it will go from high to low.

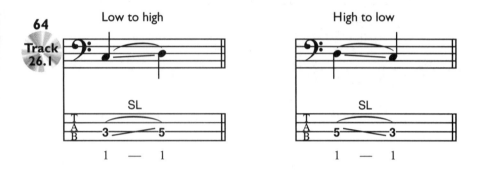

The following exercise will get each finger used to this technique by sliding each finger up in succession across the major scale pattern. Because each note is sliding upwards and then down, you only need to pluck the string once at the beginning of each measure. Use only the left-hand finger for each note in the measure that is listed.

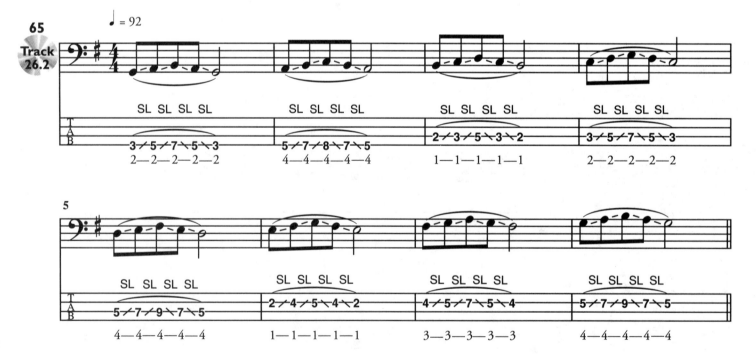

Grace Note Slides

There is another type of slide that is used in an extremely quick manner. In fact, this happens so quickly that is has no real rhythmic value and gets its own unique form of notation. This is what is known as a *grace note slide*. A *grace note* is a simple, quick embellishment to add flavor to a musical line. A tiny note is used to indicate a grace note. Below is a comparison of a grace note and an eighth note.

Eighth note: ♪

Grace note: ♪

To perform a grace note slide, you simple play the note that is to be slid from and immediately slide up or down towards your target, or main note. Your right-hand plucking and left-hand sliding should occur simultaneously.

This simple exercise below shows a grace note slide from the C on the 3rd fret of the 3rd string to the D on the 5th fret of the 3rd string. Notice that even though there are grace notes within the measure, because they have no true rhythmic value, we can still use four quarter notes.

66

Track 27.1

As a side note, another technique we can apply to grace notes is the use of hammer-ons and pull-offs. Although these are found less than grace note slides, they can add a cool sound to an otherwise dull bass line.

67

Track 27.2

7th Chord Bass Lines

The following bass lines combine all the elements we've discussed in this chapter: 7th chords, sixteenth notes, dead notes, and slides. They are designed specifically to outline 7th chords and get them in your ear.

This next reggae-style bass line uses our common fingerings for each 7th chord. It also uses another form of grace note slide known as an *unspecified slide,* which is notated with just a short ascending or descending line before the note (see measures 3 and 4). This tells you to quickly slide to the main note from one or two frets below.

This next bass line outlines a chord progression in the key of B Major that goes from the I chord (BMaj7), to the ii chord (C#min7), to the IV chord (EMaj7), and finally to the V7 chord (F#7) before going back to I.

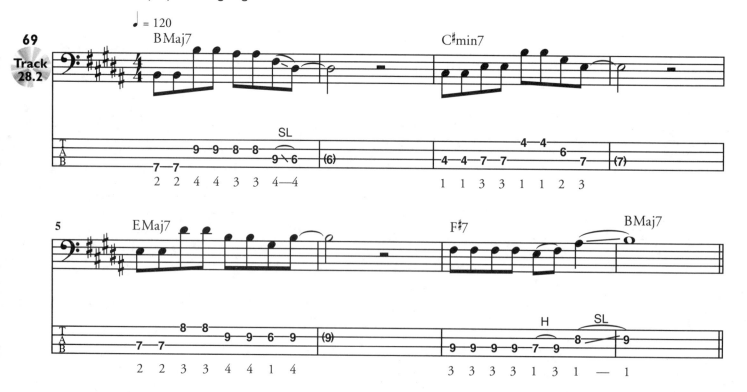

The next bass line starts by outlining an A Major 7th chord and moving up the fretboard. To make things interesting in the first two bars, when we bounce between the 3rd, 5th, and 7th of the chord, we'll play the diatonic 5th above each note (highlighted in gray). Also, note the slide in measure 6.

Each measure of this bass line uses the same exact rhythm. When we see common occurring melodies or rhythms in a piece, this type of repeating phrase is called a *motif* or *motive*. So, this bass line's rhythmic motive is two eighth notes followed by four sixteenth notes.

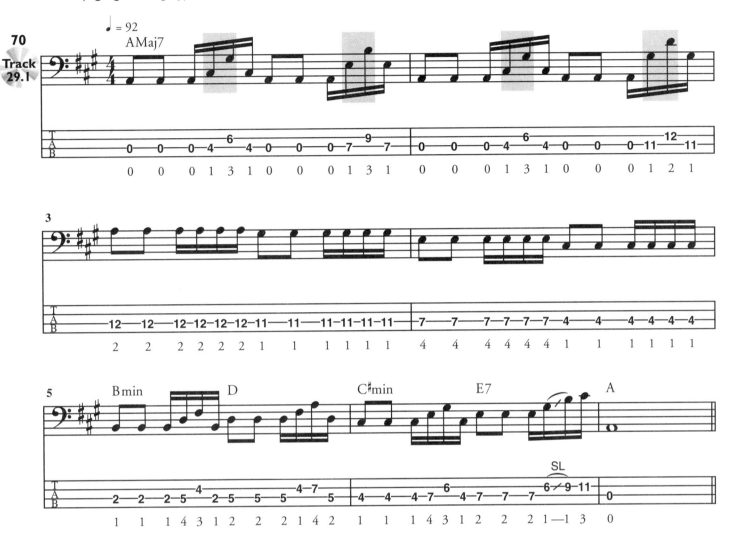

The following is a sort of prog-rock bass line that outlines two chords, and then follows by doubling the guitar riffs heard on the CD.

Chapter 6: Basic Rock Chord Progressions

A *chord progression* is, simply, a series of chords played in a particular order. A large portion of rock music follows time-tested, tried-and-true chord progressions. There are certain chord progressions that are the basis for many classic songs and styles.

Earlier, you saw how we can analyze chords by using Roman numerals; when discussing chord progressions, reading Roman numerals is an essential tool. This will allow you to identify and play chord progressions easily, and even *transpose*, or move them into different keys.

This chapter will focus on several common chord progressions, so you can get used to playing them as well as how they sound. Once you can identify chord progressions simply by the way they sound, you'll be able to build effective bass lines on the fly.

Most of these rock progressions make use of the I, IV, and V or V7 chords, because they are the only major chords diatonic to the major scale. A very common sound is of the V chord pulling back to I. The reason for this is that the V and V7 chords create tension, and we want to hear the resolution back to the I chord. When this happens at the end of a piece, or end of a phrase or section (such as a verse or chorus), it is called a *cadence*. Not all cadences go from V to I, but this is the most commonly found cadence, especially in rock music.

The I–IV–V Progression

The I–IV–V progression is one of the most basic chord progressions because it's made up of only the three diatonic major chords. First, arpeggiate through each chord in the progression to get used to the sound and the shape of the arpeggio under your fingers.

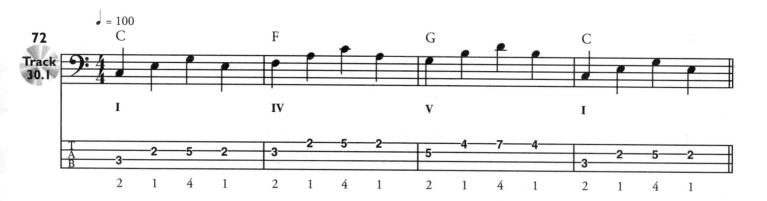

Now, by using the techniques we have learned, we can easily spice up this bass line. Also, we don't have to play every note in each chord because, very frequently, a keyboardist or guitar player will already be playing that full chord.

This next bass line uses only the root and 5th of each chord, which is a common rock bass technique, especially if the guitarist is playing *power chords*, which consist of only the root and 5th of the chord. Note that the roots of the IV and V chords are played on the 4th string.

This next example of the I–IV–V progression has a punk rock feel to it. We play the same rhythm for each chord, as well as the same pattern of intervals. As we discussed earlier, patterns or recurring ideas within music are known as motifs, or motives.

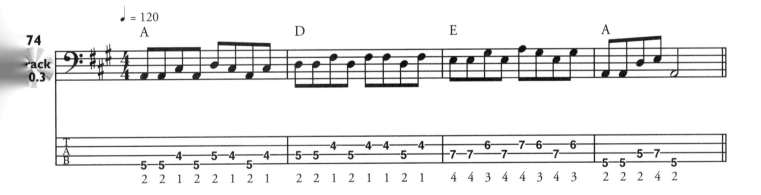

The '50s Progression: I–vi–IV–V

The I–vi–IV–V chord progression is also referred to as the '50s progression because it was used a lot by doo-wop groups in the 1950s and 1960s. However, this progression has been seen in rock settings as well, such as in "D'yer Mak'er" by Led Zeppelin, "Baby I'm an Anarchist" by Against Me!, and "Every Breath You Take" by the Police. Once again, start by arpeggiating each chord in the progression. This time, we'll start on the 8th fret of the 4th string so that reaching the vi chord will require less shifting.

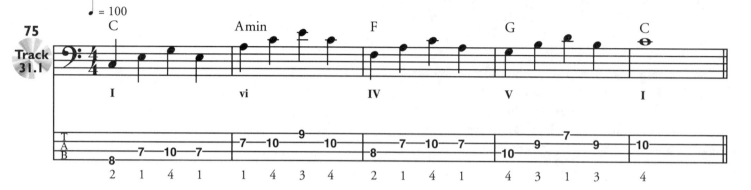

This next bass line emphasizes that 1950s doo-wop sound. It moves from chord to chord using *passing tones*, which are non-chord tones that are quickly played to move from one chord to another. If a passing tone is within the key we are playing, it's a *diatonic passing tone*. If the passing tone is not within the key, then it is a *chromatic passing tone*.

Chromatic passing tones can really add a lot of character and movement to a simple bass line, and they are always recognizable by their accidentals (sharps or flats). Notice the chromatic passing tone at the end of measure 3. This passing tone is between the root of the IV chord (F) and the root of the V chord (G).

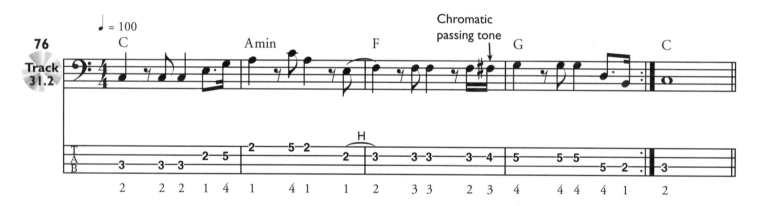

A great variation of the '50s progression involves switching the vi and the IV chords to make a I–IV–vi–V progression. This chord progression can be found in a lot of great classic rock songs, such as "More Than a Feeling" by Boston. This example changes chords every two beats. The rate at which chords change is called *harmonic rhythm*.

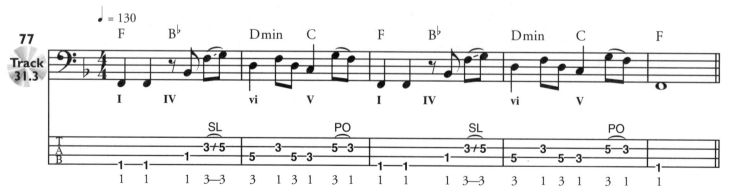

The Pop-Punk Progression: I–V–vi–IV

The I–V–vi–IV chord progression is unique because it doesn't end with our typical V–I cadence, but still sounds great when repeated. This progression has been used in countless rock songs such as "Under the Bridge" by the Red Hot Chili Peppers, "Beast of Burden" by the Rolling Stones, and "Let It Be" by the Beatles. It has also been known in more recent years as the *pop-punk progression*, because it has been used so frequently in that genre. This progression is perfect if you are looking to write a great hook. Let's start by arpeggiating diatonic 7th chords over the progression.

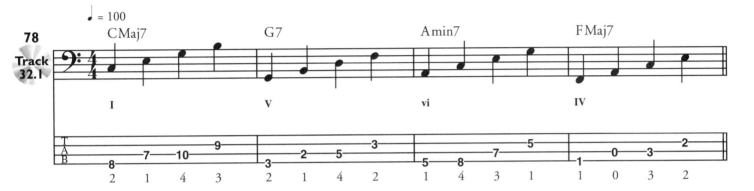

The I–V–vi–IV chord progression is used by almost all pop-punk bands. Great examples of this progression are found in "Dammit" and "Feeling This" by Blink 182 and "When I Come Around" by Green Day. The following pop-punk bass line stays mainly on the roots of each chord with some chromatic passing tones.

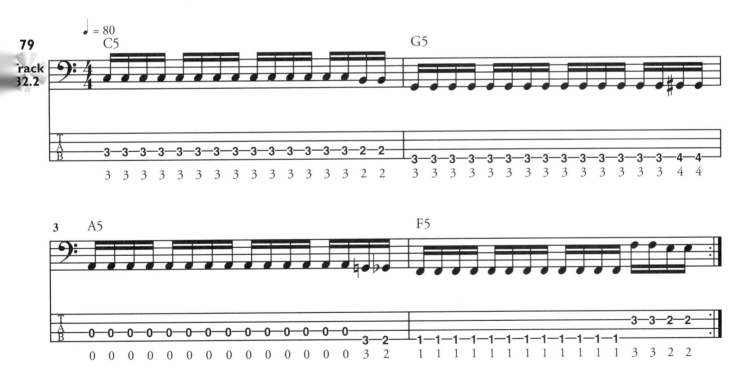

This punk bass line is in the key of E. Even though the rhythm in the last two measures is straight eighth notes, pay attention to the counting and where the octaves and 5ths are to be played.

Other Chord Progressions

There are a wide variety of chord progressions that have been used time and time again. Now that you know how to approach building bass lines off of a chord progression, take some time and come up with bass lines based on the following progressions. They can be in any key you like, and can be played in any style. Remember to first arpeggiate through the chord progression and then spice it up however you like. The point is to be able to identify which chords you need to play and also to think about how you want to move from chord to chord.

Chord Progressions
I–vi–ii–V
I–ii–iii–IV–V
I–vii°–vi–V
I–iii–vi–ii–V

Rhythm Practice: $\frac{3}{4}$ Time and Triplets

Up to this point, everything we've played has been in $\frac{4}{4}$. This is the most common time signature in Western music. However, we shouldn't limit ourselves; there are a number of different time signatures we can play in, and the next that we'll cover is $\frac{3}{4}$.

In $\frac{3}{4}$ time, each measure consists of three beats. Because there are only three beats in a measure, whole notes (which last for four beats) cannot be used. So, in order to play a note for a whole measure of $\frac{3}{4}$ time, we use the dotted half note.

$\frac{3}{4}$ = 3 beats per measure
Quarter note ♩ = one beat

Our counting and subdividing is done exactly the same as in $\frac{4}{4}$, except now we only count up to three.

Sometimes, $\frac{3}{4}$ time is referred to as *waltz time*, because it is the main time signature for waltzes and other early dance music. $\frac{3}{4}$ time is popular for dancing because it has a swaying feel to it. Below is an example of a typical waltz pattern.

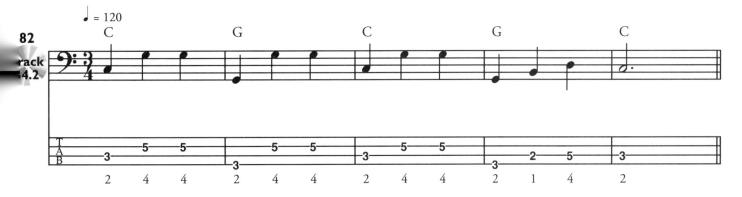

$\frac{3}{4}$ time certainly isn't limited to old dance music. It has been used in thousands of country western songs, especially ballads. But also, many modern rock bands have used this time signature for some of their most popular songs. Some examples are "Third Eye" by Tool, "3 Libras" by A Perfect Circle, "Breaking the Girl" by the Red Hot Chili Peppers, "My Name Is Jonas" by Weezer, "Hear You Me" by Jimmy Eat World, "A Wolf at the Door" by Radiohead, and many more.

The following rhythmic exercises focus specifically on playing in $\frac{3}{4}$ time. Each one uses various combinations of note values.

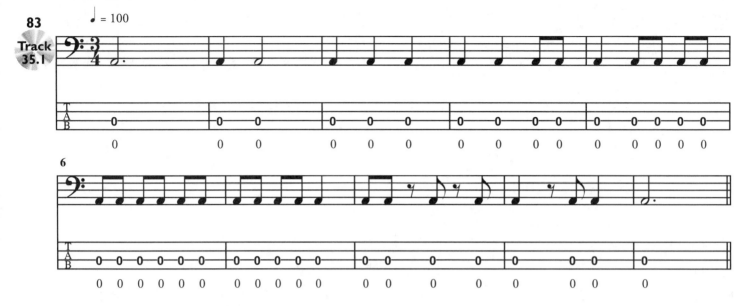

The following exercise alternates between the root and 5th, with the 5th being accented on a different beat in each measure.

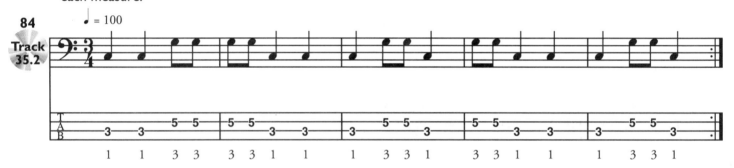

This next rhythmic exercise expands on the last idea by moving through a chord progression and putting the roots, 3rds, and 5ths of each chord on different beats.

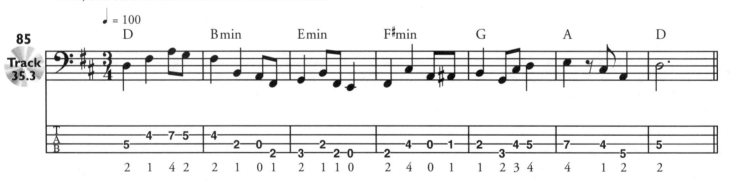

One technique that progressive rock bands use all the time is mixing, or changing, time signatures. You must be able to pay attention quickly to when the measures change time signatures. Sometimes it can be as brief as one measure. Simply prepare yourself to adjust your counting. This exercise starts in $\frac{3}{4}$ and switches after three measures to $\frac{4}{4}$.

Triplets

You just learned how the time signature can divide the measure into three beats. Up to this point, we have been dividing our note values into even halves, but we can divide these into three parts as well, just as we can a measure. When we divide a note value into three parts, we get what is known as a *triplet*. Triplets are named after the type of notes from which they are made. The most basic triplet is equal to a quarter note divided into three even parts and is called an *eighth-note triplet*.

Eight-note triplets look like three eighth notes beamed together with a 3 above them.

If you don't see the 3 above or below the beam, then these are *straight eighth notes* ("normal" duration eighth notes equal to a half beat each). Each eighth-note triplet is equal in time to one beat.

Counting triplets is more difficult than counting subdivisions of two or four. But once the concept of counting triplets is understood, it will be very easy to feel them, which will make playing them feel natural. There are two approaches to counting triplets. The first is to count "**1**-2-3, **2**-2-3, **3**-2-3, **4**-2-3." The second approach is to say the word "trip-a-let," with a syllable for each note of the triplet (see below).

Playing triplets will become much easier after you hear and feel the rhythm. You must remember that triplets are faster than eighth notes, but slower than sixteenth notes.

Try these simple triplet rhythm exercises. Be sure that the first note of each triplet comes down right on the beat.

Locking in with the Drums

As bassists, we have to face the unfortunate fact that we are not often put into the spotlight of the band (unless you're Les Claypool or Victor Wooten). A lot of what drives rock tunes tends to be guitar riffs, and time and time again, you will come across bass lines that simply echo the guitar riff, or simply play the roots of the chords the rhythm guitar is playing. Both of these are not bad ways to play by any means, but the bass is to act as the glue of the band; the bond between rhythm, harmony, and melody. And the best way to use your abilities to drive a tune is to truly tap into the idea that you are part of the rhythm section, not just a third guitar with thicker strings and a longer neck.

The most basic rhythm section of any band consists of bass and drums. In order to properly drive the music, the bass and drums must be "tight" and in sync with one another. This means more than simply just playing in time together. Rhythm section parts can have a huge impact on the feeling of a song if both bass and drums complement each other. Being able to get locked in with a drummer, to hear and feel the pulse and the beat he is playing, will allow you to create a groove that will be the backbone to the music.

To study drum beats, it helps to know how they are notated. Here is what drum notation looks like:

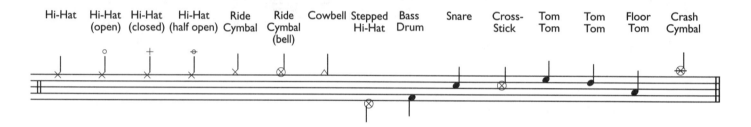

The easiest way to lock in with the drums is to listen for the kick, or bass, drum and play on every bass drum hit. More advanced ways involve creating your fills and embellishments around what the drummer might be doing on his kit. Sometimes you may even be able to play a straight rhythm of just eighth or sixteenth notes, and sync up with the drums by emphasizing certain beats with your note choice.

Classic Rock Beat

This first example will use a very basic rock drum beat. This style of beat is very common among alternative bands and classic rock bands like AC/DC. Notice that the bass drum is hitting on beat 1, the "and" of 2, and on beat 3.

In the second and fourth measures, the bass drum falls on beat 1, and the "and" of 3. These are the notes we want to emphasize.

91
Track 37.1

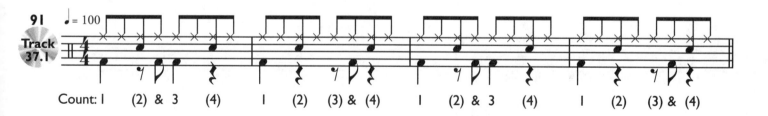

Count: 1   (2) & 3   (4)   1   (2) (3) & (4)   1   (2) & 3   (4)   1   (2) (3) & (4)

The following three bass lines fit well over the drum beat on the previous page. Once you have practiced and understand these bass lines, come up with some of your own to go along with this beat.

This bass line matches the bass drum beat exactly.

This next bass line plays the octave above the previous note each time the snare drum hits.

This third line uses a straight eighth-note rhythm, but emphasizes the bass drum hits with the C on the 3rd fret of the 3rd string, and the snare drum hits with the D on the 5th fret.

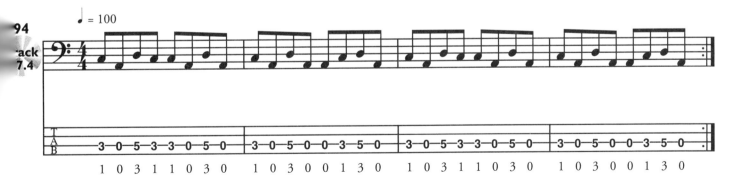

Funky Drum Beat

This funk drum beat is much more involved and much more syncopated. Because of the challenging rhythms found in funk, and the role of the rhythm section to get people to dance, having a bass player and drummer sync up together results in monumental power and groove. Check out this funky drum beat.

The following bass line will focus solely on syncing up with the bass drum. With a beat like this, it is very important to be able to subdivide accurately. Practice each measure separately at a slow tempo, then bring it up to speed. Although the notation may look rhythmically intimidating, the line becomes easier to play once you hear the drum part.

The bass line below is the same as the first, only now we will emphasize the snare drum hits as well.

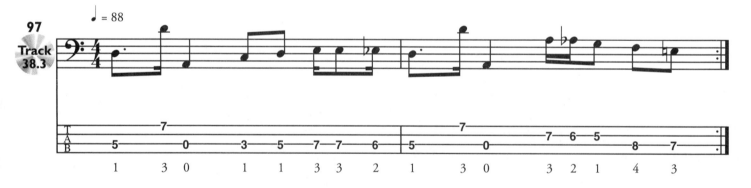

This next line features a rhythm of straight sixteenth notes, emphasizing the bass and snare hits through changing pitches. This style of funk is often referred to as *finger funk*.

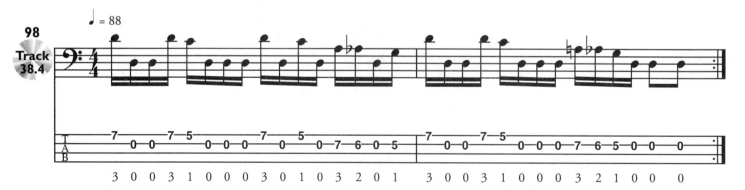

Chapter 7: New Scales

The Natural Minor Scale

Just as we have major and minor chords, we also have major and minor key signatures, and major and minor scales. The *minor scale* will give a darker sound to our bass lines.

There are three types of minor scales: *natural minor*, *harmonic minor*, and *melodic minor*. For now, we'll discuss the simplest of these scales: the natural minor scale.

The pattern of whole steps and half steps for the natural minor scale is W–H–W–W–H–W–W. Let's look at an example of an A Natural Minor scale.

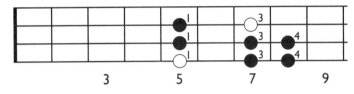

A Natural Minor Scale

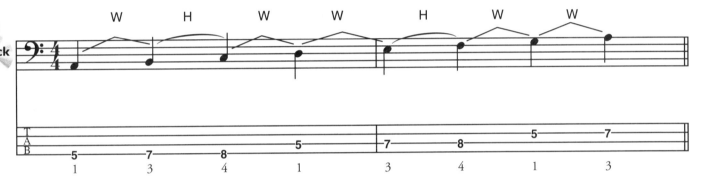

Relative Thinking

When talking about scales other than the major scale, we generally have two ways of thinking about how they are built. One way is called *relative thinking*, where we relate these scales to the major scale. The minor scale uses all the same notes as the major scale, only starting on the 6th degree of the major scale.

For example, the 6th degree in the key of C Major is A. So we can say that the *relative minor* of C Major is the key of A Minor. You can see that both C Major and A Minor share the same key signature and have no sharps or flats. You can also see that, even though they use the same notes, both have very different sounds because the order of half and whole steps has changed.

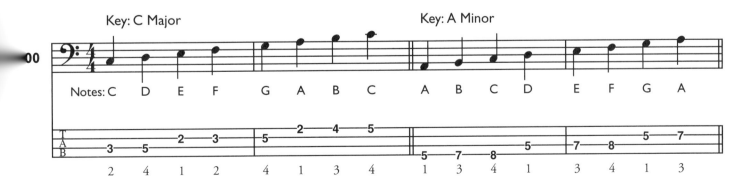

Parallel Thinking

Another way we can think about the minor scale is by comparing the minor scale with the major scale using the same root; this is called *parallel thinking*. The major scale will be our base for comparison with its scale degrees being labeled as 1 through 7.

C Major Scale

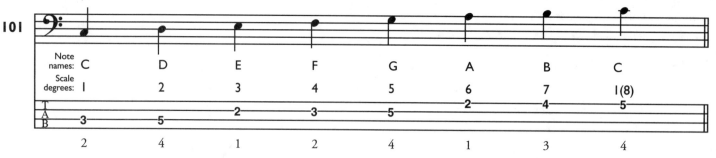

Now, let's build a minor scale from the same root (C), using the minor scale formula of whole steps and half steps. We see that, compared to the major scale, we have an E♭ instead of an E♮, giving us a ♭3 scale degree, as well as an A♭, giving us a ♭6 scale degree, and a B♭, giving us a ♭7 scale degree. So, we can say that C Natural Minor is distinguished by its ♭3, ♭6, and ♭7 scale degrees.

C Natural Minor Scale

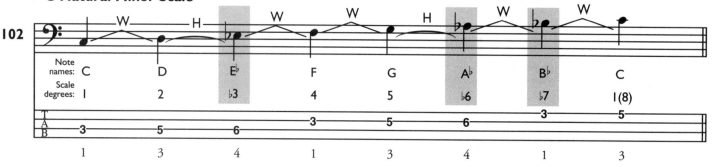

Minor Keys and Key Signatures

Because the minor scale and keys relate to the major scale, they share key signatures. However, you must remember that a natural minor key is built on the 6th degree of some major key. So the key signature for G Major is *not* the same key signature for G Minor.

If you want to find the relative minor of a key signature, you only need to go backwards three half steps, or go to the 6th scale degree that major key. So, the key signature of G Major is also the key signature for E Minor. (G, F♯, F♮, E). Following are a couple of two-octave A Natural minor scales to practice and memorize.

Two-Octave Natural Minor Scale Fingerings

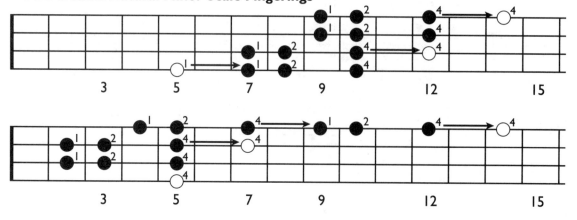

Heavy Metal Bass Lines Using the Natural Minor Scale

Because the natural minor scale has a darker, sadder sound, it's perfect for playing hard rock, heavy metal, and hardcore music. This example is a heavy metal bass line written in the key of E Minor (the relative minor of G Major), in open position. This one utilizes the galloping Steve Harris–style rhythm we discussed earlier.

The next bass line is in the key of A Minor and is played on just the 3rd string with a triplet rhythm.

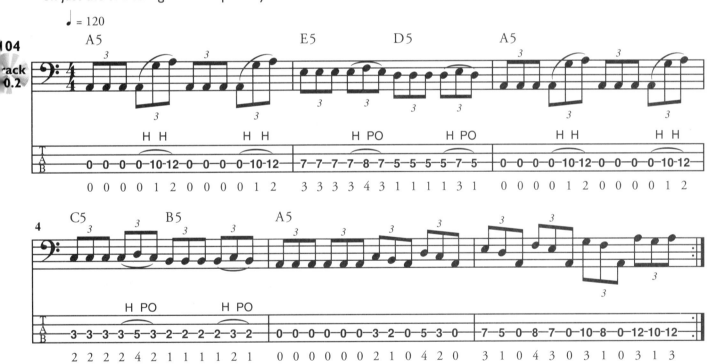

The bass line below is in the style of "N.I.B." by Black Sabbath. Be sure to check out bassist Geezer Butler's bass solo that appears at the beginning of "N.I.B." on their self-titled 1970 album, as well as Primus's version released in 2000.

The Major Pentatonic Scale

We often think that the more options we have, the better our music will be. However, one technique that can have a strong effect on the way we write music is to "limit" ourselves. By limiting the number of notes from which to choose, we can get very distinct sounds. One example of this is the use of *pentatonic scales*. "Penta" is a prefix meaning five (like pentagon or pentagram), and "tonic" means tones or notes, so we have a five-note scale.

There are many different types of pentatonic scales from around the world, each with their own unique sounds. One of the most common in popular music is the *major pentatonic scale*. It's used in many forms of rock music because it sounds great and can be played over any major triad or major 7th chord.

The major pentatonic scale has the same construction as the major scale, but has no 4th or 7th scale degrees (see below).

C Major Pentatonic Scale

Here are a couple of fingering patterns for the major pentatonic scale.

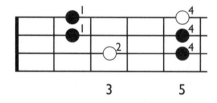
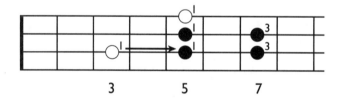

The major pentatonic scale has a very distinct bright and happy sound. The reason for this sound is that because there are no 4th or 7th scale degrees, there is no longer a dissonant tritone found within the scale.

Two-Octave Major Pentatonic Fingering

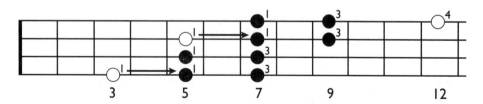

Major Pentatonic Bass Lines

This bass line has a Motown feel to it.

This bass line is in the style of Van Morrison's hit "Wild Night."

This '80s pop-rock bass line is in the style of "Just What I Needed" by the Cars. This fingering for the major pentatonic scale is very demanding on the fingers, so be sure to stretch out before trying this one. If you find you can't do it, take some time and figure out how you could play this in an open position.

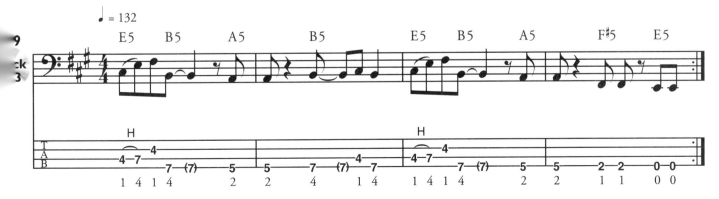

The Minor Pentatonic Scale

The *minor pentatonic scale* is possibly the most widely used scale by rock musicians. It is also used very heavily in the blues. Just like when learning the natural minor scale, we can think about the minor pentatonic scale in both relative and parallel ways.

The relative way would be to say the minor pentatonic scale is simply the major pentatonic scale, starting from the 6th scale degree. Or, we can think of it as the natural minor scale without its 2nd or ♭6th scale degrees.

110
Track 43

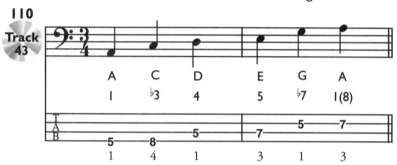

Below are some fingerings for the minor pentatonic scale.

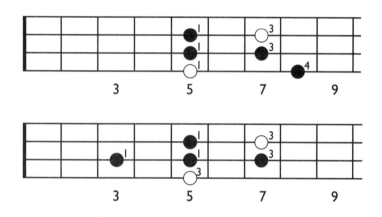

Two-Octave Minor Pentatonic Fingerings

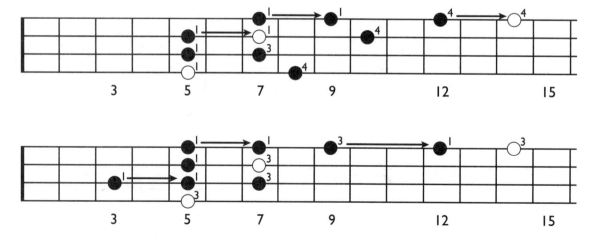

Minor Pentatonic Bass Lines

The minor pentatonic line below is in the style of "Bombtrack" by Rage Against the Machine. Rage is known for blending rock, funk, and hip-hop influences, and they frequently used the pentatonic scale because of its common use in different genres.

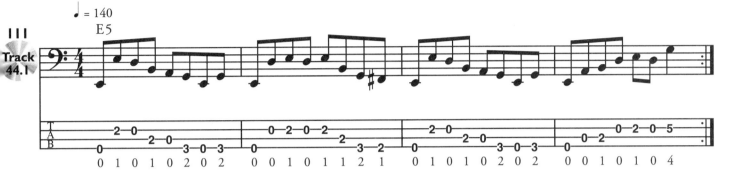

The next line is based on the blues and uses the minor pentatonic scale over each chord. Our scale shape will move with the roots of the chords, so we'll be playing a different minor pentatonic scale over each chord. In other words, over the Gmin7 chord, we'll be playing a G Minor Pentatonic scale; over the Cmin7 chord, the C Minor Pentatonic scale, etc. For more on the blues, see Chapter 8 (page 79).

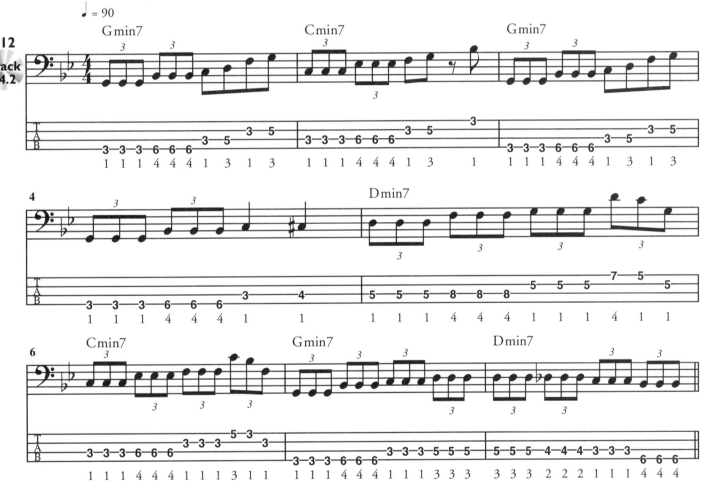

Here's one more for you that quickly runs off the two-octave minor pentatonic fingering.

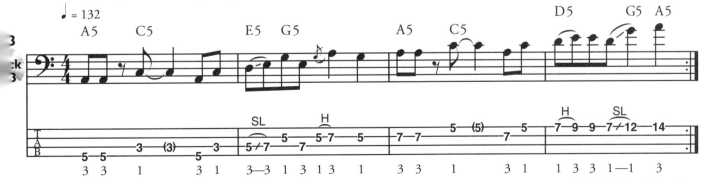

Rhythm Practice: Swing Eighths

Swing eighth notes are also known as *swing eighths* or *shuffle eighths*. Unlike regular, or straight, eighth notes, swing eighths have a different feel for each note in a pair of eighth notes. You are sure to recognize this feel and sound. In a pair of swing eighth notes, the first eighth note is held slightly longer than the second.

The easiest way to break down this feel is to think of triplets with the first two notes of the triplet tied together. This will be the rhythm for swing eighths.

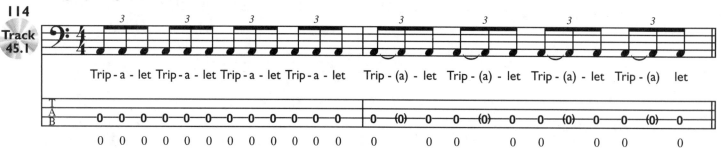

Swing eighths are notated exactly the same as straight eighths, although they are usually beamed in groups of two rather than four. Usually, you'll see *Swing 8ths* written at the beginning of a piece where swing eighths are required.

Try playing up and down the G Minor Pentatonic scale using swing eighths, playing one note of the scale per measure.

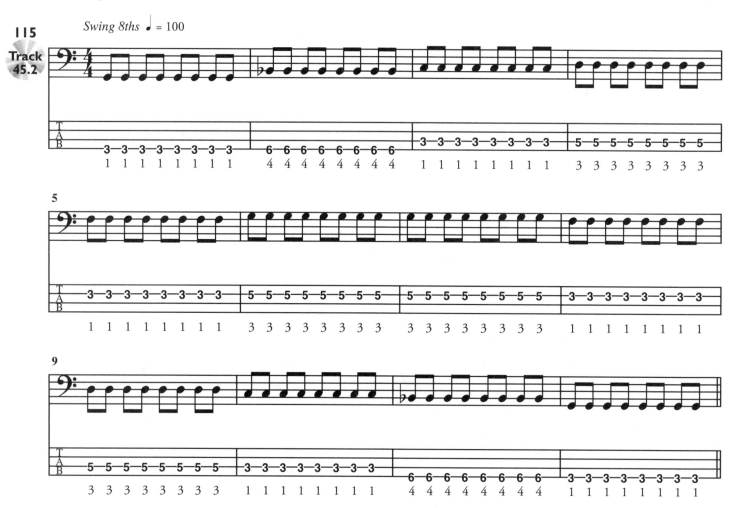

Being able to play swing eighths is essential to playing certain styles of rock music that are influenced by blues and jazz. This feel should be fairly simple to grasp once you have it under your fingers, and you'll easily be able to recognize when it is appropriate to use this rhythm.

Chapter 8: The Blues

The blues is the basis for many types of music, including rock and roll. There are many great rock bands that are heavily influenced by the blues, such as Led Zeppelin, the Beatles, and countless Southern rock bands. Knowing how to play the blues is essential to being a versatile rock bassist.

The 12-Bar Blues

One of the most important aspects of a blues composition is the form of the song, the most common being the *12-bar blues*. This a 12-bar progression that, in its most basic form, uses only three chords: the I, IV, and V chords. The progression consists of three 4-bar sections, and almost all 12-bar blues progressions follow the same pattern of chords shown below.

Basic 12-Bar Blues Progression

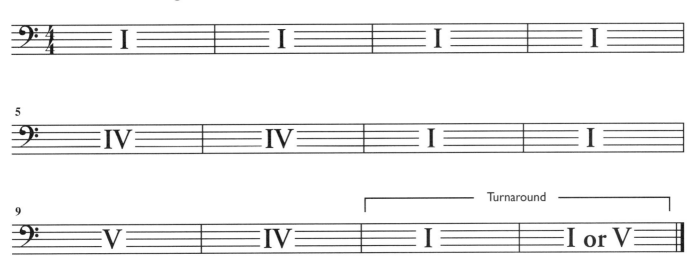

You can see that the first 4-measure section is played completely on the I chord. The second 4-measure section plays two measures of the IV chord, and then two measures of the I chord.

The third 4-measure section starts with one measure of the V chord, which is followed by one measure of the IV chord. The final two bars are known as the *turnaround* because it turns the progression back around to repeat, or signals the end of the tune. This section starts on the I chord. The second measure of the turnaround can be played with either the I chord or the V chord.

Most often, blues songs will repeat this same 12-bar section over and over again with changing lyrics. When repeated, the V chord should be played in bar 12 because this creates a tension-and-release cadence, whereas for the final progression, you can simply end on the I chord.

Basic Blues

The following is a basic 12-bar blues bass line written in the key of A Major. We'll play each chord as a triad. Don't forget to swing those eighth notes!

Track 46 *Basic Blues in A*

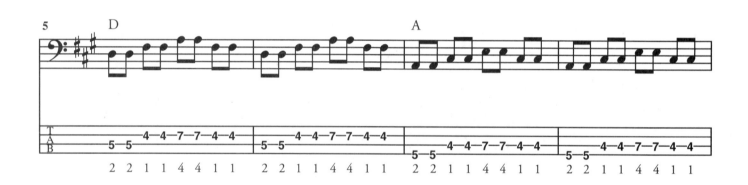

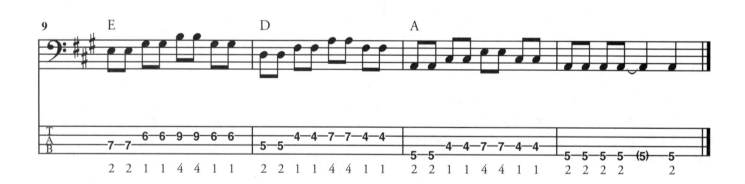

Dominant 7th Blues

The previous bass line outlined the basic 12-bar blues pattern, but it lacked a bluesy sound. Because we were simply playing major triads for each chord, the major 3rd created a happy, upbeat sound, which is rarely heard in blues tunes.

The blues tends to cast aside traditional rules of music theory in order to facilitate the feel, sound, and emotion of the blues. With this being said, more often than not, you'll find each chord played as a dominant 7th chord. When this is the case, it really adds a bluesy sound to your bass line to play the ♭7 of each chord.

This bass line follows a typical pattern known as a *boogie pattern*. We omit any 3rd the chord may have, and even though the progression is still I–IV–V, each chord is a dominant 7th.

Track 47 *Dominant Boogie Blues in F*

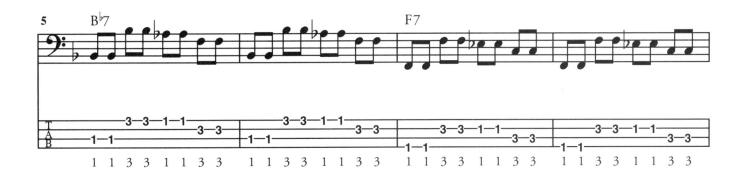

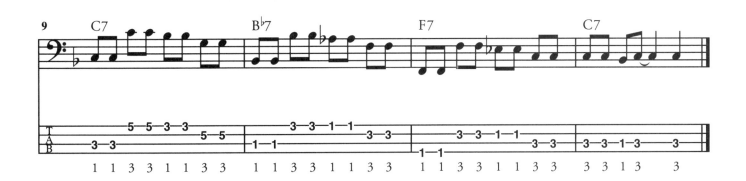

The Quick Change

Another common trick used in the first line of a 12-bar progression is the *quick change* (or *quick four*), which is simply going to the IV chord for the second bar. This next bass line will use dominant 7th chords and the quick change. The pattern used is in the style of the blues standard "Messin' with the Kid," which was originally recorded by Junior Wells in 1960. Since then, this song has been recorded by the Blues Brothers, Buddy Guy, Johnny Winter, Freddie King, and even AC/DC. Each version has a different bass line, but they all have a similar flavor. The main idea is to play the root, 5, and ♭7, and always end the chord on the octave. Now, if you are doing some impromptu jamming with some friends or at an open mic with some strangers, when someone says "12-bar in the style of 'Messin' with the Kid' " (or sometimes just referred to as "The Kid"), you'll know what to do.

This process is very common with blues recordings. Very often, one song will be done by many people, so if you find a tune you like, do some research and see how other bass players approach it. Be sure to listen the Blues Brothers version with Duck Dunn on bass, then be sure to find other songs Duck has played on as well. Make sure you play this example with straight eighth notes.

Track 48 *Quick Change Blues in G*

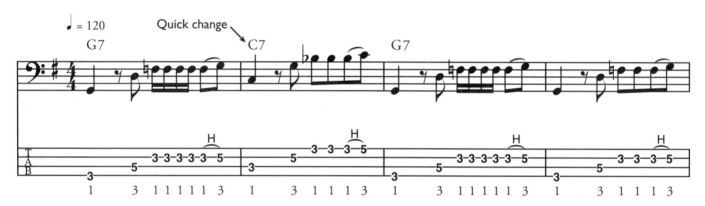

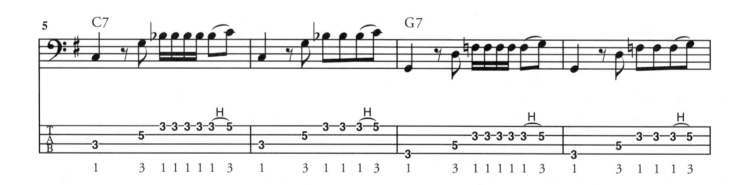

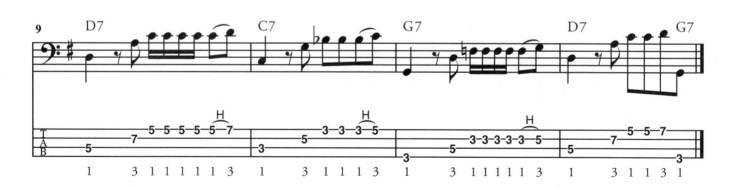

Minor Blues

Another form of the blues that has a really low-down, mysterious, and sad feeling to it is the *minor blues progression*. Rather than being based on major triads or dominant 7th chords, it's based around minor 7th chords. We can play the minor pentatonic scale over each chord.

To really add to that low-down, sad feeling, minor blues songs tend to be slower in tempo. Pay attention to the rhythm in the last measure of the turnaround. There are grace-note hammer-ons before each triplet.

Track 49   *C Minor Blues*

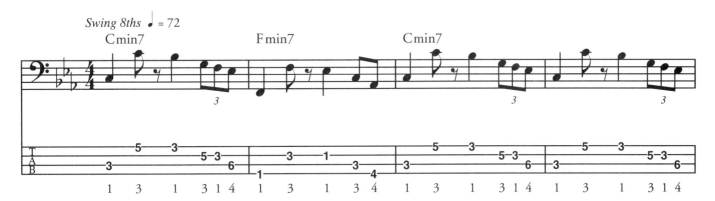

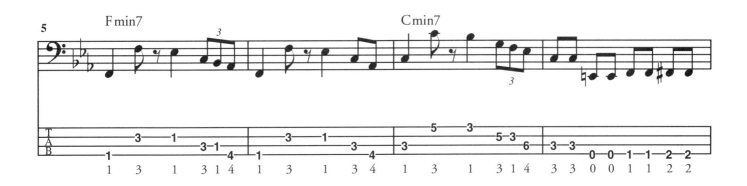

The blues is a truly American form of music that is responsible for the birth of so many other musical genres. With its history comes many variations and styles that you should do your best to check out. The examples in this chapter are just some of the most common and basic ideas used in the blues genre. There are *8-bar* and *16-bar* blues forms, as well as blues in other time signatures and feels. In fact, did you know that some of the earliest blues musicians didn't even pay attention to the form? The number of bars could be 10, 13, 15, or however long it took to sing the lyrics.

The Blues Scale

To really get that blues sound into your bass lines, you need *blue notes*. These are notes with a minor quality, such as the ♭3 and ♭7 of the minor pentatonic scale, played over a major or dominant 7th chord. When you add the ♭5, another blue note, to the minor pentatonic scale, you get the *blues scale*.

A Blues Scale

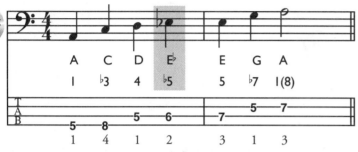

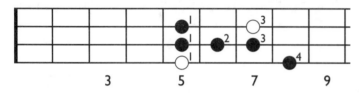

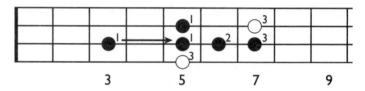

Two-Octave Fingering

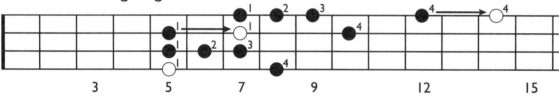

Many of the greatest classic rock bands were influenced by the blues, including Pink Floyd, Creedence Clearwater Revival, and the Beatles. Perhaps the most heavily blues-influenced rock band is Led Zeppelin, and it is an undisputed fact the John Paul Jones is one of the greatest rock bassists of all time.

Not only did Zeppelin use the blues form in many of their tunes, but John Paul Jones utilized the blues scale to create some great riffs. This two-chord vamp is in the style of "Heartbreaker" and uses the G Blues scale.

To truly experience John Paul Jones' mastery of the blues sound, be sure to listen to "The Lemon Song" on *Led Zeppelin II*.

The blues scale is a great tool for writing awesome riff-based lines. As long as the guitar is either playing the same riff as you or playing minor, dominant 7th, or power chords, this scale will work. Check out these next few blues scale riffs.

The example below bounces off the 4th string while using the E Blues scale. Notice how using straight eighths instead of swing eighths gives this blues-based line a more driving, rock edge.

Most bass lines using the blues scale only tend to utilize the ♭5 of the scale as a quick passing tone; however, when you focus on playing that note more, you can create a dark and eerie sound that's full of tension created from the tritone, the interval between the tonic (D) and the ♭5 (A♭).

Here's another riff that is in the style of Rage Against the Machine's "Bombtrack." This bass line is in the style of the main verse riff, and uses the F♯ Blues scale.

Chapter 9: Modes of the Major Scale

This diagram maps out the C Major scale played across the top three strings, and all the way up to the 17th fret. We will use this map of the major scale to discuss *modes*.

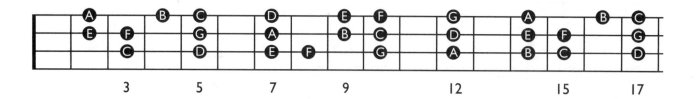

To put it simply, modes are different ways of playing the same scale to give us different sounds. If you play up and down the notes of C Major scale, starting on any pitch within it, you will be playing a mode of the major scale. Each mode has a specific name and tonal characteristics that make each one unique.

The Ionian Mode

The first mode of the major scale starts on the tonic of that scale and is called the *Ionian* mode. This is the same exact scale as our standard major scale. Using the map of the modes, we would start with our 2nd finger. However, you can play the Ionian mode using any of the fingerings of the major scale.

Ionian is considered a *major mode* because of the major 3rd interval between the root and the 3rd scale degree. There are only three major modes that occur diatonically in the major scale: Ionian, Lydian, and Mixolydian, just as we saw that there are only three major chords diatonic to the major scale: the I, IV, and V chords.

C Ionian

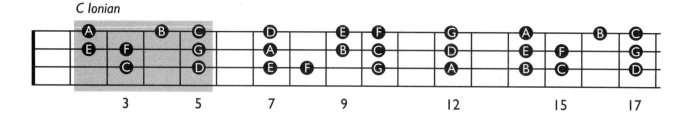

C Ionian

121
Track
52

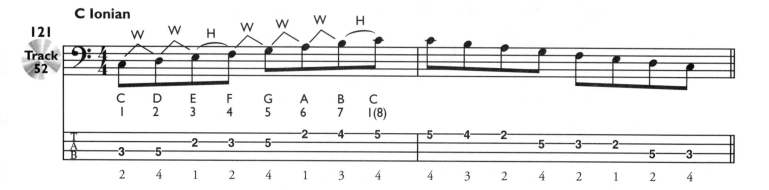

The Dorian Mode

Dorian is the mode built on the 2nd scale degree, which would be D in the key of C Major. A tune that uses predominantly the Dorian mode is said to be "in the Dorian *modality*," rather than a major or minor "key." When playing Dorian, notice that it has a minor sound to it, even though we are still using only notes from the C Major scale. Because the Dorian mode's 3rd scale degree is a minor 3rd from the D tonic, it is called a *minor mode*.

Because this mode is based on the 2nd scale degree of the C Major scale, it fits perfectly over the ii chord, which would be Dmin or Dmin7.

D Dorian

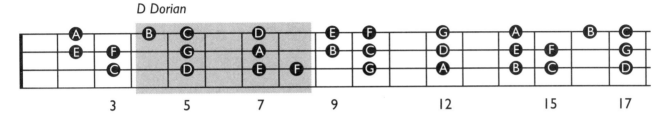

For this fingering of the Dorian mode, be sure to use your 4th finger to play the 5th of the mode in order to be able to grab the 6th with your 1st finger. You can see that the pattern of whole steps and half steps for the Dorian mode is W–H–W–W–W–H–W.

One way to analyze modes is by using parallel thinking (see page 72). This means comparing the mode to a different scale or mode starting on the same note. Comparing D Dorian and D Major, we see that the Dorian mode has a ♭3 and ♭7. We can also compare the Dorian mode to the natural minor scale and see that the Dorian mode has a ♮6.

D Dorian

122
Track
53.1

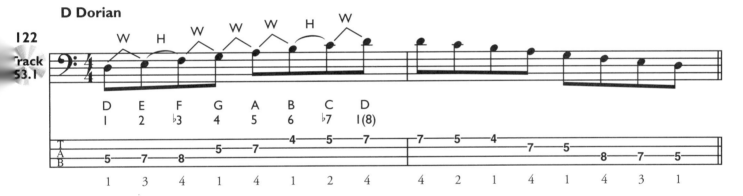

Take some time now to use your knowledge of tetrachords, the major scale, and its fingerings to figure out some additional fingerings for the Dorian mode.

The Dorian mode has been used in popular rock songs such as "Eleanor Rigby" by the Beatles, "Light My Fire" by the Doors, and "Another Brick in the Wall" by Pink Floyd.

In the example below, pay attention to the finger shift in measure 2 with the sixteenth-note hammer-ons. Rather than using your 1st and 3rd fingers, you'll hammer-on from your 1st to your 4th finger.

23
ack
.2

The Phrygian Mode

Phrygian is the mode built on the 3rd scale degree, which would be E in the key of C Major. As with the Dorian mode, a song that uses predominantly the Phrygian mode is said to be "in the Phrygian modality." (This concept applies to all the modes.) Like Dorian, the Phrygian mode has an interval of a minor 3rd between its tonic and 3rd scale degrees, making it a minor mode as well.

Because this mode is based on the 3rd scale degree of the C Major scale, it fits perfectly over the iii chord, which would be Emin or Emin7.

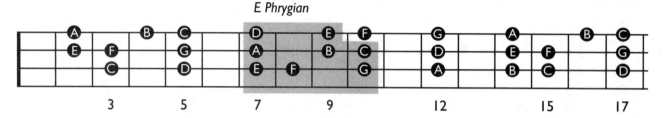

E Phrygian

This fingering for the Phrygian mode starts with the 1st finger on the 3rd string, 7th fret (E) and requires no shifting. You can see that the pattern of whole steps and half steps for the Phrygian mode is H–W–W–W–H–W–W. We can think of the Phrygian mode as a natural minor scale with a ♭2.

E Phrygian

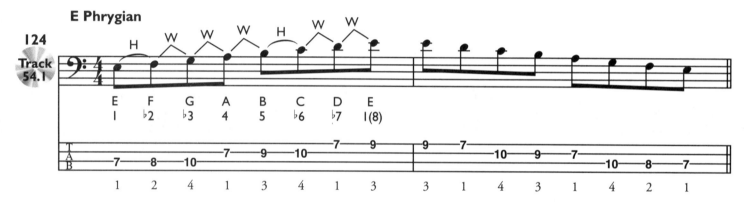

Take some time now using your knowledge of tetrachords, the major scale, and its fingerings to figure out some additional fingerings for the Phrygian mode.

The Phrygian mode has been used in popular rock songs such as "White Rabbit" by Jefferson Airplane and "Set the Controls for the Heart of the Sun" by Pink Floyd.

This Phrygian bass line has strong heavy metal feel to it.

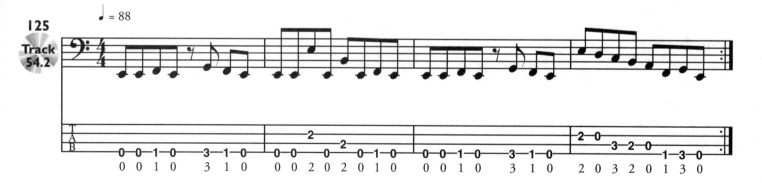

The Lydian Mode

Lydian is the mode built on the 4th scale degree, which would be F in the key of C Major. Notice that Lydian has a major 3rd interval between the tonic and 3rd scale degrees, making it a major mode.

Because this mode is based on the 4th scale degree of the C Major scale, it fits perfectly over the IV chord, which would be F or FMaj7.

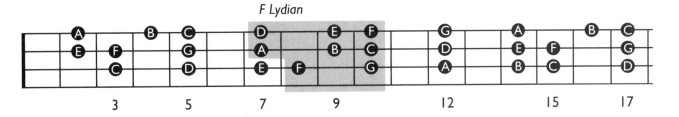

This fingering for the Lydian mode starts with the 2nd finger on the 3rd string, 8th fret (F) and requires no shifting. You can see that the pattern of whole steps and half steps for the Lydian mode is W–W–W–H–W–W–H. We can think of the Lydian mode as the major scale with a ♯4.

F Lydian

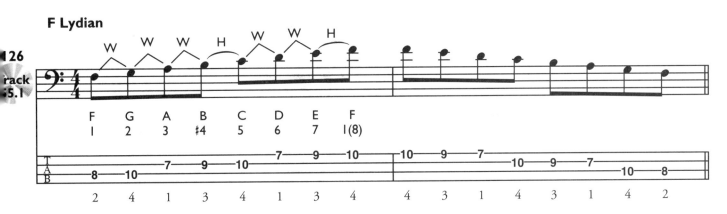

Take some time now to use your knowledge of tetrachords, the major scale, and its fingerings to figure out some additional fingerings for the Lydian mode.

The Lydian mode has been used in popular rock songs such as the intro to "Dancing Days" by Led Zeppelin. This bass line is in the style of the verses to "Man on the Moon" by R.E.M.

The Mixolydian Mode

Mixolydian is the mode built on the 5th scale degree, which would be G in the key of C Major. Notice that Mixolydian has a major 3rd interval between the root and 3rd scale degrees, making it a major mode.

Because Mixolydian is based on the 5th scale degree of the C Major scale, it fits perfectly over the V chord, which would be G or G7.

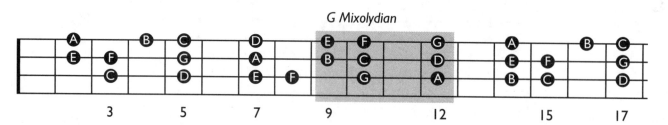

This fingering for the Mixolydian mode starts with the 2nd finger on the 10th fret (G) and requires no shifting. You can see that the pattern of whole steps and half steps for the

Mixolydian mode is W–W–H–W–W–H–W. We can think of the Mixolydian mode as the major scale with a ♭7.

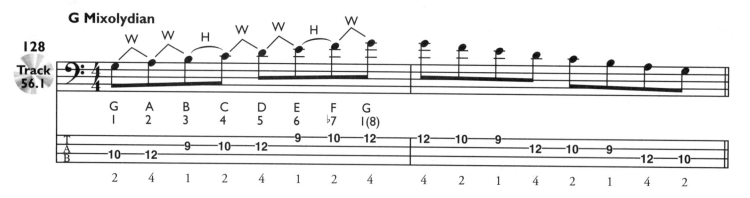

Take some time now to use your knowledge of tetrachords, the major scale, and its fingerings to figure out some additional fingerings for the Mixolydian mode.

The Mixolydian mode is very common in rock music and has been used in popular songs such as "Evenflow" by Pearl Jam, "I Feel Free" by Cream, "Sympathy for the Devil" by the Rolling Stones, "Jane Says" by Janes Addiction, and "Sweet Child o' Mine" by Guns N' Roses.

The Aeolian Mode

Aeolian is the mode built on the 6th scale degree, which would be A in the key of C Major. The Aeolian mode is exactly the same as the natural minor scale, so we can use all the same fingerings.

Because this mode is based on the 6th scale degree of the C Major scale, it fits perfectly over the vi chord, which would be Amin or Amin7.

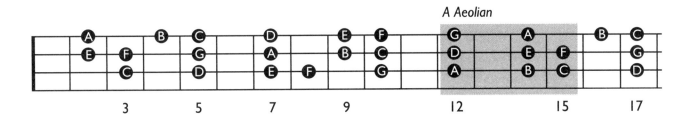

This fingering for the Aeolian mode starts with the 1st finger on the 3rd string, 12th fret (A) and requires no shifting. You can see that the pattern of whole steps and half steps for the Aeolian mode is W–H–W–W–H–W–W.

A Aeolian

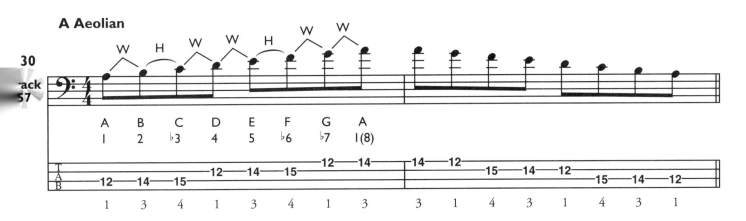

Take some time now to using your knowledge of tetrachords, the major scale, and its fingerings to figure out some additional fingerings for the Aeolian mode.

The Locrian Mode

Locrian is the mode built on the 7th scale degree, which would be B in the key of C Major. You have probably noticed a pattern that each mode corresponds to the chords built on its scale degree, so because this mode is based on the 7th scale degree of the C Major scale, it fits perfectly over the vii° chord, which would be B°, Bmin7♭5, or Bø7.

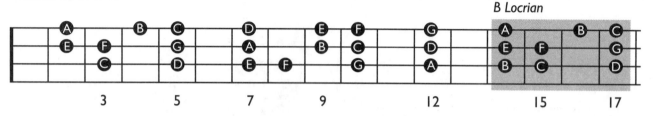

This fingering for the Locrian mode starts with the 1st finger on the 3rd string, 14th fret (B) and requires no shifting. You can see that the pattern of whole steps and half steps for the Mixolydian mode is H–W–W–H–W–W–W. We can think of the Locrian mode as the natural minor scale with a ♭2 and a ♭5.

B Locrian

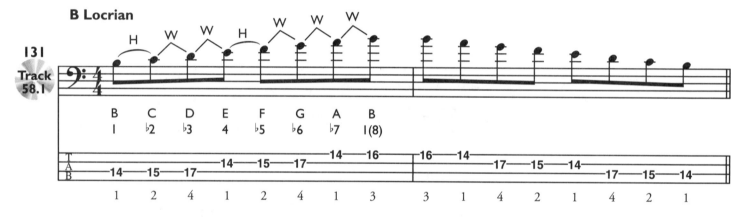

Take some time now to figure out some additional fingerings for the Locrian mode.

The Locrian mode is very popular with heavy metal and metalcore bands (and even industrial and techno groups) due to its dissonant sound. A couple of popular examples of the use of the Locrian mode are the main riff from "Painkiller" by Judas Priest and "Army of Me" by Björk.

The following bass line has a great dissonant sound that comes from focusing on the tritone found within the Locrian mode.

Modal Warm-Up

Now that you are familiar with the feel and sound of each mode, you should focus on blending the modes within your bass lines. This modal warm-up exercise will take you through each diatonic mode in the key of C, with the tonic of each mode located on the 3rd string. Each mode will alternate direction, with one ascending, and the next descending. Once you reach the Ionian mode an octave higher, the pattern reverses.

Next to each chord symbol is the name of the mode you are playing. Be sure to say each one aloud as you play through it.

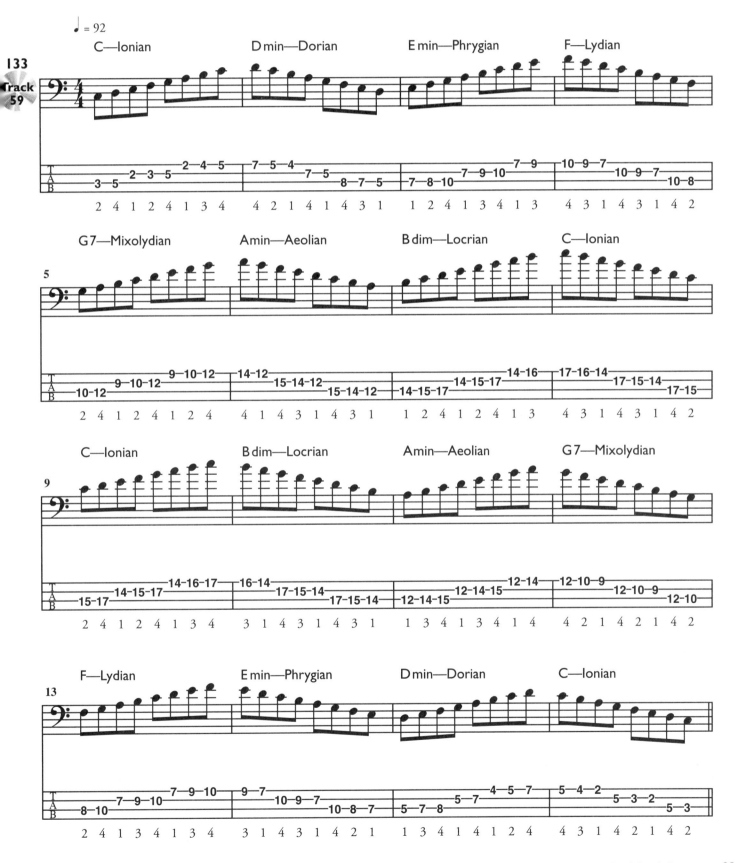

Modal Bass Lines

This first line is in the style of the intro to "Sweet Child o' Mine" by Guns N' Roses. Although Guns N' Roses are known for their intense energy and driving rhythm, this tune starts off with a very melodic bass line set in D Mixolydian. Duff McKagan's bass line stays around the 12th fret area of this mode. If you really want to try and get that Duff tone, try playing this one with a pick.

This example uses a *pickup* measure, which is an introductory measure containing fewer than the full number of beats indicated by the time signature. Using a pickup measure allows us to write bass lines that do not start on beat 1.

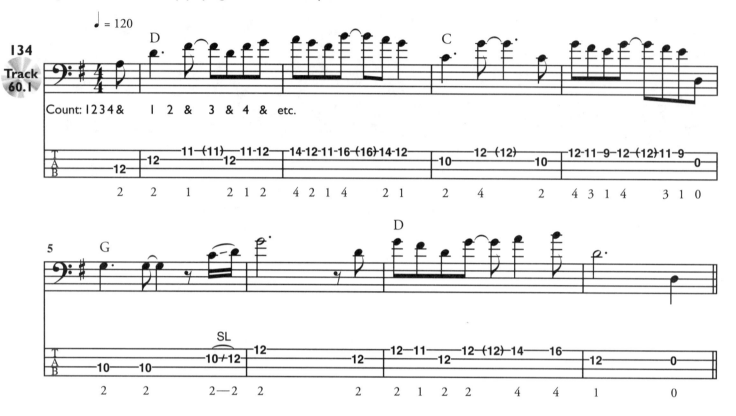

The next bass line is in the style of "Bury Me with It" by Modest Mouse. This bass line is in F♯ Phrygian. "Bury Me with It" actually uses pretty much the same two-bar bass line for the entire song.

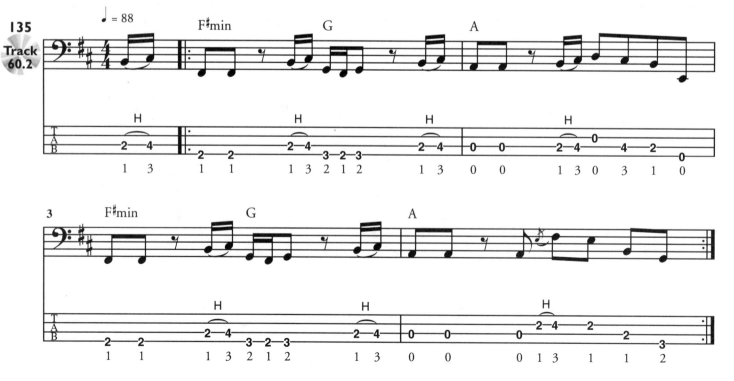

This repeating bass line in E Dorian, is in the style of "Riders on the Storm" by the Doors. The Doors used the Dorian mode more frequently than most other bands. What makes this bass line Dorian is the emphasis on the natural 6th.

This bass line is in the style of "Come Original" by 311 and uses the Lydian mode. Combined with the syncopated rhythm, this creates a very bright and upbeat mood to the song.

Building Modes of Other Scales

Now that you understand how modes are constructed, you can easily apply them to other scales that you know, as well as ones you will learn in the future. For instance, to create the modes of the natural minor scale, all you would have to do is start with the Aeolian mode, since it's the same as the natural minor scale, and work your way upwards in order. Modes are a great way to not only compliment and outline chords, but to add variety to your writing as well.

Modes of the Major Pentatonic Scale

Just as with the major scale, you can use modes to play the major and minor pentatonic scales as well. A lot of guitar players refer to different positions of the pentatonic scale as "box patterns," but basically these are just different modes of the pentatonic scale.

Because the major pentatonic scale is made of only five different notes, there are going to be only five modes. This diagram maps out each mode in C Major Pentatonic across the fretboard.

Modes of C Major Pentatonic

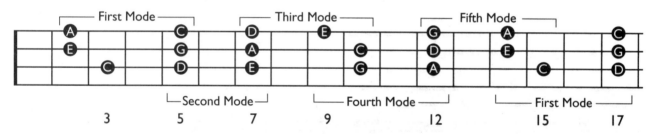

Being able to play all the modes fluidly on their own and together will allow you to play the major scale, or its relative minor scale, all over the neck of the bass. This will help to expand your creativity with creating riffs, fills, and even solos. This will also open up options for you when outlining chords. You will know exactly what notes you can play other than just the 1, 3, 5, or 7 of the chord.

Chapter 10: Double Stops

When we learned about intervals (page 28), we learned there are two types: melodic and harmonic. Bass players most often play melodic intervals, moving from pitch to pitch, one note at a time. However, bassists can use a type of harmonic interval known as a *double stop* to beef up their bass lines and add harmony to single-note lines.

A double stop is simply two pitches played at the same time. This is also known as a *diad*. Double stops are not technically chords (because they consist of only two notes), but we can still use them to create harmony.

Right-Hand Technique

There are several techniques for playing double stops. If you play mainly with a pick, all you need to do is strum the two adjacent strings, just as a guitar player would play a chord. However, if you don't use a pick, you want to work on plucking two strings at the same time using both your 1st and 2nd fingers. The key is to get both strings to sound at the same volume and the same time.

Another right-hand technique is to strum using the fingernail of your 1st finger. You want to pinch your thumb and 1st finger together, as if you were holding a pick, and strum down making contact with the strings

using the nail of the finger. Upstrums are more difficult to execute using this process, because there is no nail. But with time, calluses will develop on your index finger, and the hardened skin will not get damaged in this process and will still sound good.

Practice this exercise to find which technique may work best for you. Whether you are using a pick or fingernail to strum, be sure to use alternate picking on the offbeats. Again, make sure each note sounds at the same time, and has even volume.

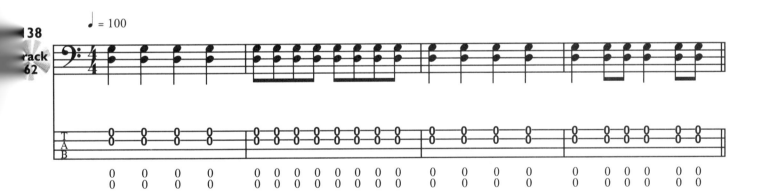

Double-Stop Fingerings

The simplest double stops to play are played across two adjacent strings. These first examples will use the 1st finger to play the root of the double stop.

Perfect 4th

This fingering shows two options of playing the interval of a perfect 4th with the root on G. You can either barre the two adjacent strings with your 1st finger or use your 1st and 2nd fingers. For an open string perfect 4th, simply play any two adjacent strings open.

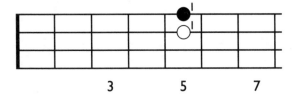

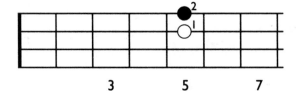

Tritone

This double stop is not used as commonly as others because of its dissonant sound. However, when used in the right context, it can add a powerful sound to any heavy metal or hardcore bass line.

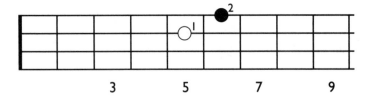

Perfect 5th (The Power Chord)

This double stop is often known as a power chord to guitarists. This is one of the most common double stops. You can play the top note using either your 3rd or 4th finger.

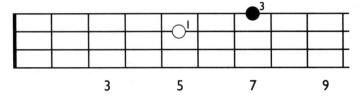

Minor 6th

This double stop is rarely used, due to the required stretching it takes to play it.

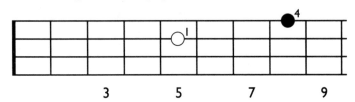

Major 3rd

This is another one of the most commonly used double stops. It uses the 2nd finger on the root.

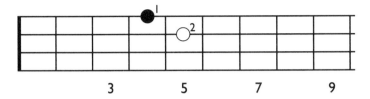

| 3 | 5 | 7 | 9 |

Minor 3rd

This common double stop uses the 3rd finger on the root.

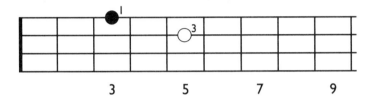

| 3 | 5 | 7 | 9 |

Major 2nd

This is another uncommon double stop due to its stretch.

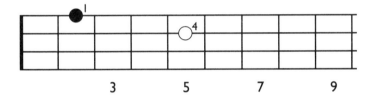

| 3 | 5 | 7 | 9 |

Playing double stops may cause strain on the hand at first, but with slow, accurate practice, you will build the strength necessary to be able to play these double stops and smoothly integrate them into your bass lines. Use this exercise to get used to each fingering. Make sure each note sounds clear and clean.

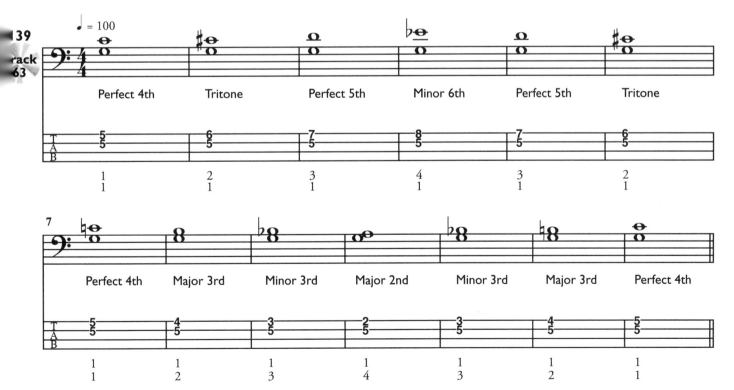

Diatonic Double Stops

Just like with chords, we have diatonic double stops that stay within the key. The following exercises will have you play up the C Major scale on the 3rd string and harmonize each note with a diatonic double stop. We'll start with 3rds, then 4ths, then 5ths.

3rds

Remember that the 3rd of a chord is what gives the chord its harmonic quality of either major or minor. These double stops will follow the same order of major and minor as our chords did. So, the only major 3rds occur on I (C), IV (F), V (G), and the octave (C).

M3 = Major 3rd
m3 = minor 3rd

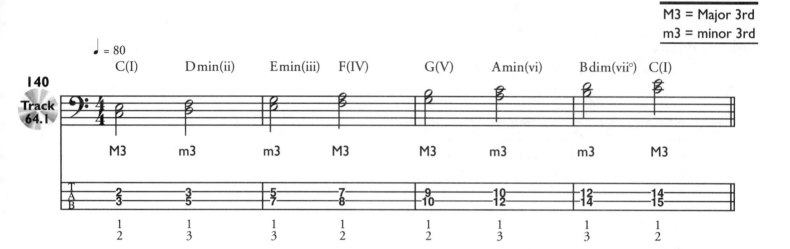

4ths

All the 4ths will be perfect, except for our IV chord (F), which has an augmented 4th (which is enharmonic to a diminished 5th).

P4 = Perfect 4th
+4 = Augmented 4th

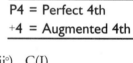

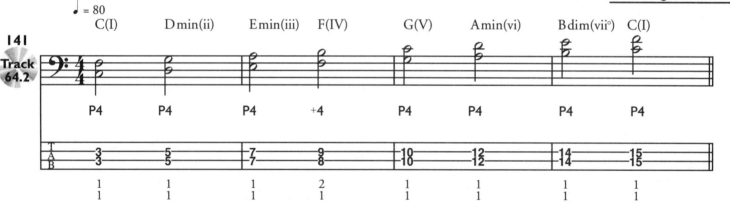

5ths

All the 5ths will be perfect, except for the vii chord (B), which has a diminished 5th.

P5 = Perfect 5th
°5 = Diminished 5th

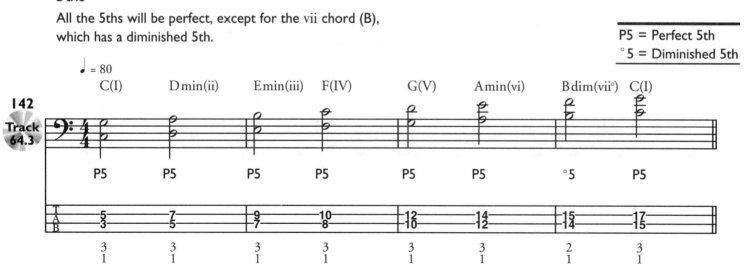

Bass Lines Using Double Stops

The following bass lines use nothing but double stops.

This one will follow our pop-punk I–V–vi–IV progression, using only our perfect 5th double-stop fingering. Try

playing this one with a pick to get it up to a fast tempo and really get a hard attack on the notes.

This next bass line is in the style of the intro to "By the Way" by the Red Hot Chili Peppers. It is played fairly quickly, so the best way to execute this one is to use a pick.

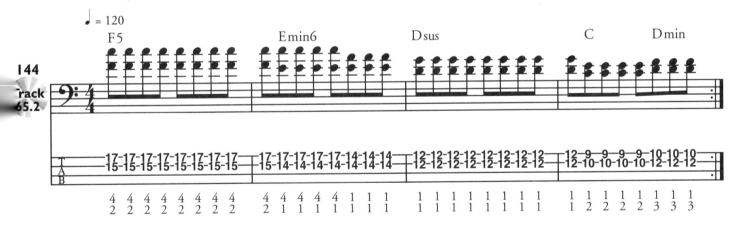

This short line below shifts between our 5th, 4th, and 3rd shapes on a single root. Be sure to play the root with your 2nd finger so you can grab the major 3rd.

Pedal Tones

A *pedal tone* is a repeated or ringing note underneath changing harmonies, kind of like a drone. This note doesn't change, but the chords or melody above it do. This a great way to add depth and tension to a piece.

As bassists, we most often play either the root or the 5th in the key of the song while the guitar or keyboard changes chords. This gives the listener something identifiable to grab on to, while the guitar or keyboard can play just about anything they want. When we do change the note we are playing, the effect is much more powerful. A great example of this is the very end of "A Day in the Life" by the Beatles, where the orchestra builds up tension, but the bass plays a pedal tone, and then everyone hits the same chord.

The following example demonstrates this concept. Although the bass line may not be too exciting to play, the overall effect it creates with the changing chords is where the real power comes in.

The chord symbols are examples of *slash chords*. The chord before the slash is what the guitarist or keyboardist would play. The letter after the slash is the note the bassist plays.

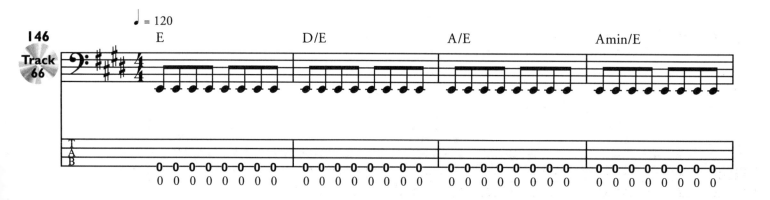

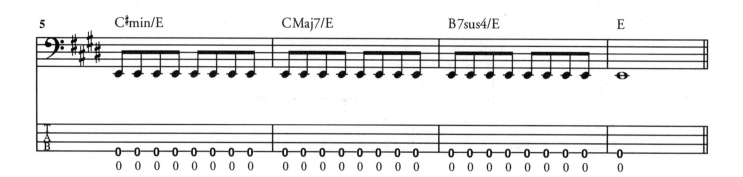

Pedal Tones Within the Bass Line

Using pedal tones is a great way for bassists to create a fuller sounding bass line, one that can hold its own without the need for another backing instrument. The ability to play a pedal tone and a bass line is a great technique to have. Several examples of this include Justin Chancellor's bass lines for "46 and 2" and "Schism" by Tool, and especially Les Claypool's haunting bass line on "Southbound Pachyderm" by Primus.

A different right-hand fingering approach may be required to play in this style. When pedaling on one string and playing the melody on an adjacent string, alternating each finger should be no problem. However, when we consistently pedal on the 4th string but play the melody on the 1st or 2nd string, it may be easier to assign each finger to a string. You would use your 1st finger for the 4th-string pedal tone, and your 2nd finger for the bass line or melody. This will also allow the pedal tone to ring more and have more of a droning effect.

Practice using this technique with the exercise below. We will play the E Natural Minor scale in 7th position while pedaling on our open 4th string. Remember to try and let the low E ring as much as possible.

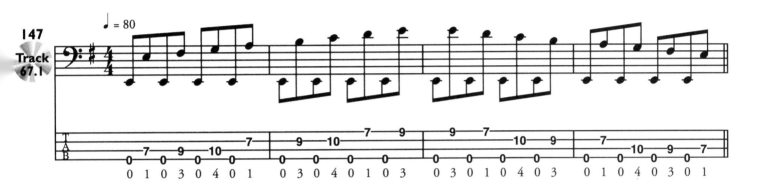

The next bass line is a great example of this technique and is in the style of "Southbound Pachyderm" by Primus. Be sure to let each fretted note ring throughout the beat. This will really separate the melody from the pedal tone and create the effect of two instruments.

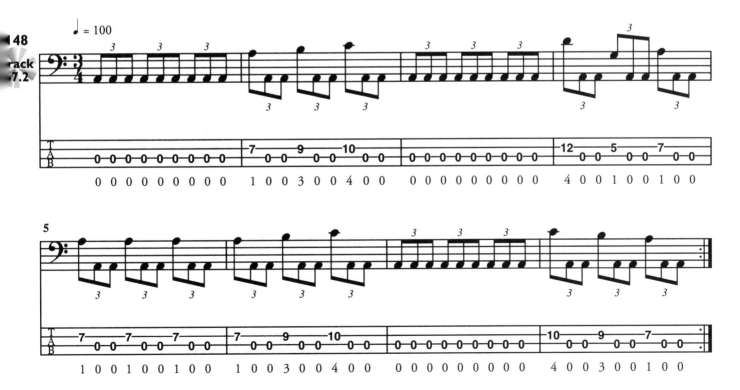

Combining Pedal Tones with Double Stops

A great way to create solo bass lines is to use a pedal tone in conjunction with double stops. However, this makes our right-hand fingering more challenging (if we are not using a pick). An effective technique is to take a fingerstyle guitar approach and use the right-hand thumb (notated with the letter *p*) to play the pedal tone and our 1st and 2nd fingers to pluck the double stops. You want to make sure your hand is relaxed and that your fingers pull inward toward your palm.

This exercise uses our 4th-string pedal tone with a progression of diatonic double stops on the higher strings. The chord progression is I–IV–I with a quick V–IV–I turnaround.

149

Track 68

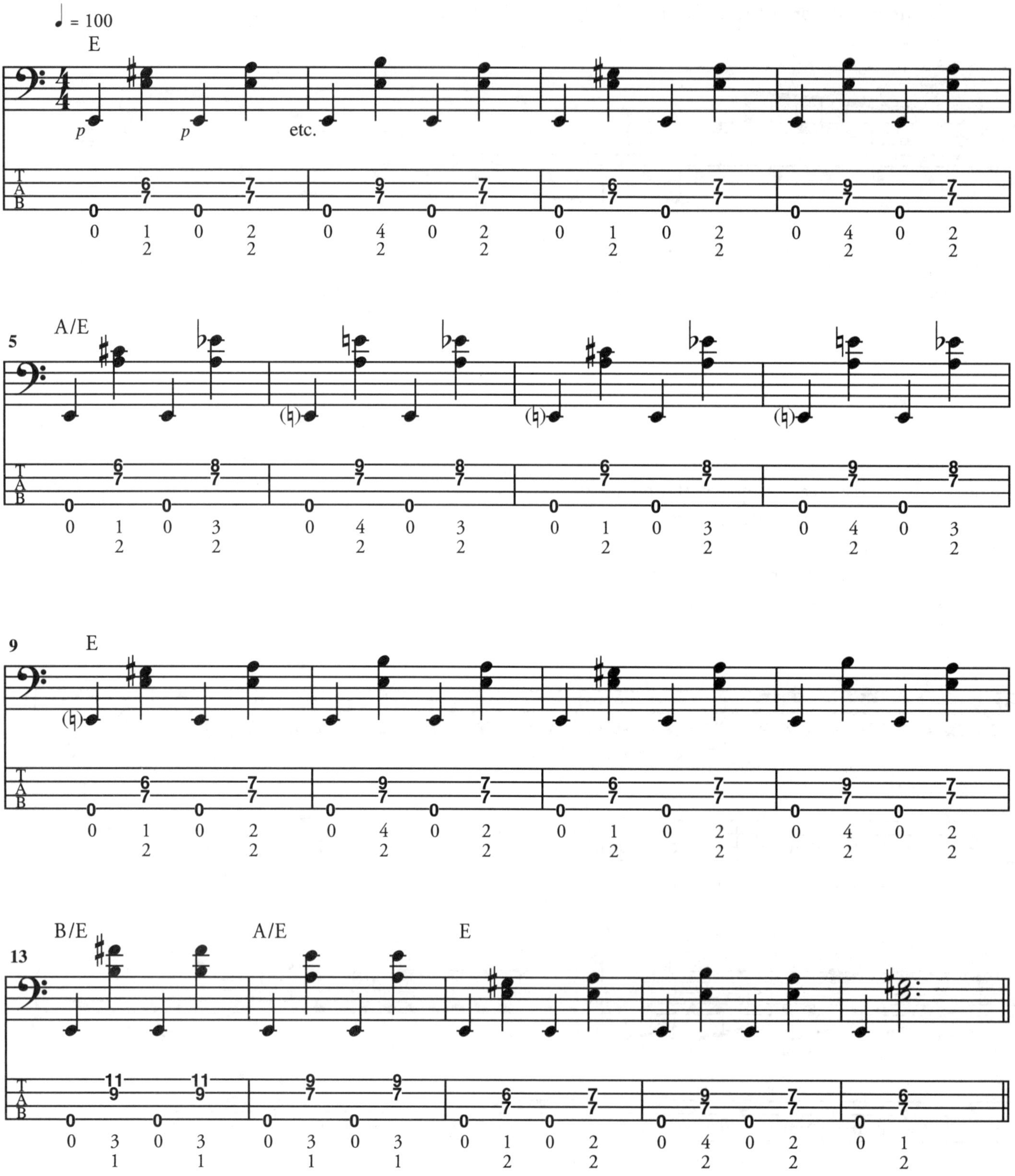

Chapter 11: Odd Time Signatures

We've talked about several time signatures, such as $\frac{4}{4}$, $\frac{3}{4}$, $\frac{6}{8}$, and $\frac{12}{8}$, but for the most part, we have been playing in $\frac{4}{4}$. However, one of the ways musicians can add uniqueness to their music is through the use of *odd time signatures*. This is a big trait of progressive rock bands such as Yes, Rush, Dream Theater, and Pink Floyd, as well as technically driven metal bands such as Tool, Meshuggah, and the Dillinger Escape Plan.

When playing odd time signatures, it is very important to count and pay attention, because you can't naturally "feel" the beat like you may be able to do with $\frac{4}{4}$. This is extremely important when songs alternate between various time signatures.

Playing in $\frac{5}{4}$

When counting odd time signatures, we can break up the meter into sections. For $\frac{5}{4}$ time, we have five beats to the measure, with the quarter note receiving one beat. Depending on the phrasing of the bass line, we can either count up to five, or we can divide it into 2+3 or 3+2. Examples of songs in $\frac{5}{4}$ include "Rosetta Stoned" by Tool, "Do What You Like" by Blind Faith, "Hangin'

Tree" by Queens of the Stone Age, and perhaps the best known song in $\frac{5}{4}$ time, the jazz classic "Take Five" by Dave Brubeck.

This first $\frac{5}{4}$ bass line can easily be counted in straight five because it consists of straight quarter notes.

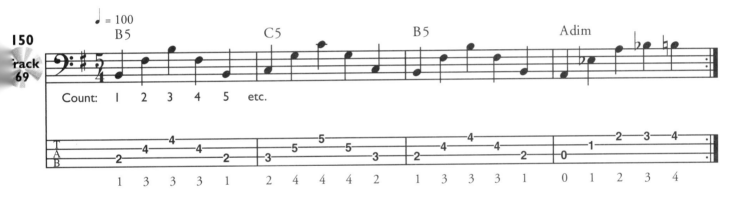

This next bass line is in the style of the line Rick Grech played on Blind Faith's "Do What You Like." Coincidentally, his bass line is also very similar to the repeating bass vamp in Dave Brubeck's "Take Five." Be sure to listen to the full version of "Do What You Like" to check out Rick Grech's

bass solo, and make sure any drummers you know listen to Ginger Baker's drum solo that immediately follows.

This line has a distinct feel, but if need be, it can be counted as 3+2, as shown by the dotted line in the first measure.

This eerie $\frac{5}{4}$ bass line is played using the Locrian mode.
Each measure can be counted as 3+2.

Playing in $\frac{7}{4}$

$\frac{7}{4}$ is another popular odd time signature. Often, the measures are counted as either 3+4 or 4+3. Occasionally, you may encounter a piece that is not easily divided up, and may feel more comfortable counting straight seven. In this case, you can easily count by saying this easy-to-remember, seven-syllable phrase: "I-Like-To-Play-In-Sev-en."

1	2	3	4	5	6	7
I	-Like	-To-	Play	-In	- Sev	- en

Some popular rock songs in $\frac{7}{4}$ time include "Solsbury Hill" by Peter Gabriel, "Ticks and Leeches" by Tool, and perhaps the most commercially successful, best-known song in $\frac{7}{4}$ time, "Money" by Pink Floyd.

This first bass line is in the style of "Money" and is a great example of how to create a groove using an odd time signature. Each measure of this bass line can be counted as 3+4.

This $\frac{7}{4}$ groove is counted as 4+3.

This next bass line is in the style of the intro to "Ticks and Leeches" by Tool. This one switches between measures divided as 4+3 and 3+4. Be sure to count carefully for the syncopation in the second measure.

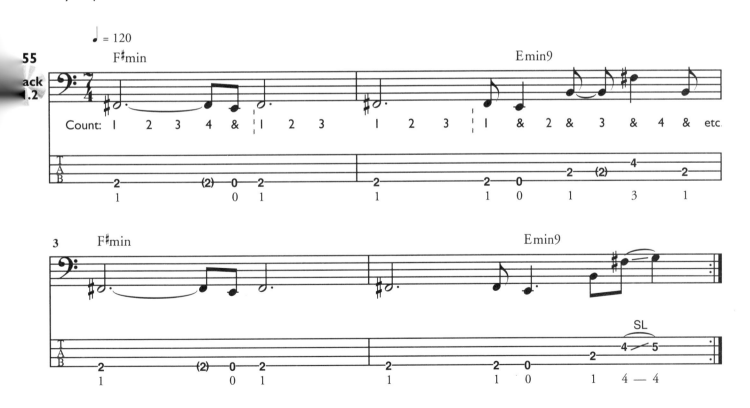

Playing in $\frac{7}{8}$

With $\frac{7}{8}$ time, the beat is given to the eighth note, so this time signature has a much faster feel to it. However, because this is an odd time signature, it becomes difficult to count using our standard eighth-note subdivision. We would not have an even amount of numbers and "&s." This kind of time signature makes breaking up beat patterns essential. It will be much easier to count "1-2-3, 1-2-3-4; 1-2-3, 1-2-3-4" rather than trying to loop "1-&, 2-&, 3-&, 4; 1-&, 2-&, 3-&, 4." (See example below.)

This first bass line is in straight eighth notes. Notice that they are beamed in groups of two, three, and four notes. As long as a group of three beamed notes does not have a bracket with a 3 over it, it isn't a triplet. These are notated like this to show the easiest way to break down the beat pattern.

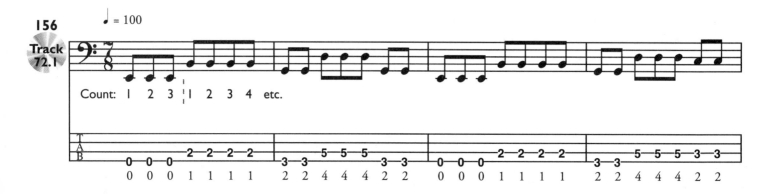

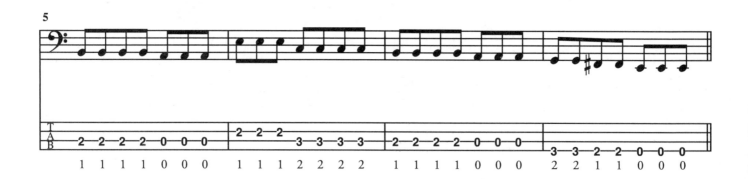

The following bass line mixes our rhythmic values and can be divided as 1–2–3–4, 1–2–3, except for measures 5 and 6 which are 1–2–3, 1–2–3–4.

Count: 1 2 3 4 ¦ 1 2 3 etc.

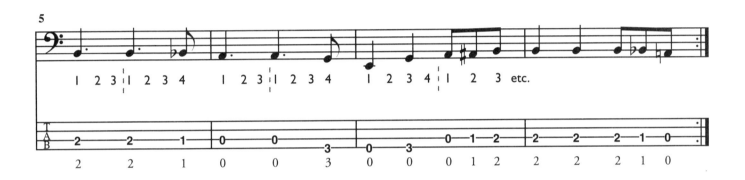

1 2 3 ¦ 1 2 3 4   1 2 3 ¦ 1 2 3 4   1 2 3 4 ¦ 1 2 3 etc.

There are certainly more odd time signatures, and some bands have been known to write songs in $\frac{11}{8}$, $\frac{13}{8}$, $\frac{15}{8}$, and more. Once you get into these larger time signatures, what determines the time signature is the phrasing of each part. Certain phrases will have certain feels that you will recognize as being in a particular time signature. Other times, you may just see a string of straight eighth or sixteenth notes, and the easiest way to count them is in a bizarre odd time signature.

The chart to the right shows various ways to break down certain time signatures. These are not hard and fast rules, but suggestions. Remember, because our natural rhythm and meter is in a series of fours, then it's recommended that four should be the largest count when breaking down beat patterns.

Time Signature	Beat Breakdown
$\frac{3}{4}$	1 2 3
$\frac{5}{4}$ and $\frac{5}{8}$	1 2 3 4 5
	1 2 3 - 1 2
	1 2 - 1 2 3
$\frac{7}{4}$ and $\frac{7}{8}$	1 2 3 4 - 1 2 3
	1 2 3 - 1 2 3 4
	1 2 - 1 2 3 - 1 2

Compound Time Signatures

What determines whether a time signature is a *compound time signature* is the top number. If the top number can be evenly divided by three, then it is a compound time signature. The most common compound time signatures use an 8 for the bottom number, giving the eighth note the beat; for example: $\frac{6}{8}$, $\frac{9}{8}$, and $\frac{12}{8}$.

Now, it is certainly okay to play these time signatures as they are written, using the top number as the number of beats per measure and the bottom number to determine what note is equal to one beat. However, because these time signatures move quickly through the eighth notes and are made of large numbers that are divisible by three, there is a unique way to interpret these time signatures.

Because the top number is divisible by three, this means that now our beat will be denoted by a dotted note. In the case of the three time signatures mentioned above, it will be a dotted quarter note. So when counting the beat in $\frac{6}{8}$, rather than counting from one to six, we simply count "1, 2" and give the eighth notes a triplet feel (see the following example).

158
Track 73.1

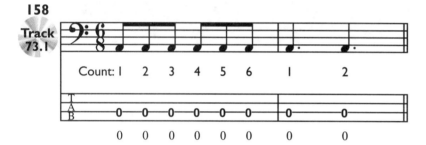

Because of this way of interpreting compound time signatures, the top number and bottom number no longer represent what they used to. Now, in order to get the number of beats per measure from the top number, we must divide by three (6 ÷ 3 = 2 beats per measure) and to get the note that receives one beat, we take the note value of the bottom number and triple its note value (eighth note x 3 = dotted quarter note).

Understanding compound time signatures is much more complicated than actually playing them. Their feel will certainly be recognizable to you, and they are quite easy to grasp and execute.

This first line is in $\frac{6}{8}$ and is similar to part of "I Want You (Shes's So Heavy)" by the Beatles. Remember to count it with a two feel.

159
Track 73.2

This next line is in $\frac{9}{8}$ and has a "three" feel to it, meaning it can be counted as having three beats per measure. This one uses the '50s I–vi–IV–V progression.

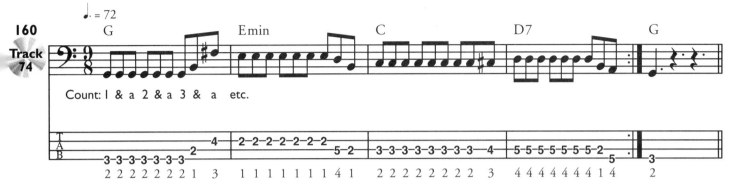

This bass line in $\frac{12}{8}$ uses a four count and is in the style of Hubert Perry's bass line on James Brown's "I Don't Mind." This example uses a *first ending* and *second ending,* indicated by a bracket with the number 1 or 2 (measures 8 and 9). The first time through, play up to the repeat sign at the end of measure 8. The second time through, skip measure 8 (the first ending) and play measure 9 instead (the second ending).

This long progressive rock example is designed to get you thinking about the practice of using different time signatures in one piece. The rhythms of the piece have been kept simple to allow for easier counting during the odd times. Notice that the catchiest riffs have been kept in straight $\frac{4}{4}$ time.

Track 76 *Dissonant Time*

Chapter 12: Slap & Pop

One of the most popular techniques amongst all electric bass players is *slap bass*. Slap bass has a unique percussive feel that is effectively used in many forms of rock music. This is the result of the strings hitting the fretboard with great intensity, which produces louder and more distinctive sounds.

Sly and the Family Stone bassist Larry Graham is credited as the originator of slap bass. He came upon the technique while trying to emulate the sound of the drums in a temporarily drummer-less band. Slap bass has since come a long way, with virtuosos like Les Claypool, Flea, and Victor Wooten taking it to new levels.

Slapping

The technique of *slapping* requires hitting the strings very hard with the right-hand thumb. The easiest way to develop the correct right-hand technique for this is to stick your arm out straight, and make a nice, big "thumbs up." Then, rotate your wrist 90 degrees inward, and bring your hand to your bass. Your thumb should be pointing straight towards the headstock. When slapping, you want to conserve energy by rotating your wrist, not pulling the whole hand away from the bass. Do this is in a quick motion, hitting the strings with enough force to get the desired sound, and be sure to bounce back off of the string. You should only bounce half an inch at the most. (See photos below.)

Preparing to slap.

Slap follow-through.

It's important to be conscious of how relaxed or stiff your right hand is. If you are getting a dull thud, instead of a crisp slap sound, then your right hand may be either too loose, which means it's absorbing the vibrations of the strings, or it may be too tight and causing strain on your arm. After practicing the slapping technique for a little while, you are sure to find a happy medium.

There are several variations on slapping. Some bassists prefer to slap through the string and rest the thumb on the string below that (see Figs. 1 and 2), while others prefer to have their thumbs almost at a 90 degree angle pointing upwards (see Figs. 3 and 4) . Some bassists even use their fingers to slap as well (see Figs. 5 and 6). However, no matter what the technique, the goal is all the same: to get the crispest, most percussive sound, with maximum comfort.

Fig. 1: Preparing to slap "through" the string.

Fig. 2: Completion of slap "through."

Fig. 3: Preparing with thumb at 90 degree angle.

Fig. 4: Follow-through with thumb at 90 degree angle.

Fig. 5: Preparing to use fingers to slap.

Fig. 6: Finger-slap follow-through.

A note that is supposed to be slapped is indicated with an upper-case S above the standard music notation. Practice the following exercises to get used to the feel of slapping the strings. Each note should ring with nearly the same volume and have the same attack.

In this first exercise, slap half notes and ascend the major scale. You may notice that when you first start slapping, you're accidentally hitting adjacent strings. This may be because of the angle of your thumb. Be sure to target the string with the thick bone of your thumb. One technique for muting the other strings is to slightly lay the palm of the right hand down on the strings not being played.

Staccato

We use hammer-ons, pull-offs, and slides to play smoothly, or legato. The opposite of legato is *staccato*, which means short and detached. Being able to play staccato is key to playing slap & pop bass lines. You want your notes to sound, but not ring out for their full values. A note to be played staccato will have a dot above or beneath its notehead ($\dot{\downarrow}$ or $\dot{\rho}$).

Occasionally, entire songs are to be played staccato, so they simply say "staccato" at the beginning of the piece.

The trick to playing staccato is to be able to quickly, smoothly, and accurately mute your notes with either the right or left hands. Try playing this slap exercise using all staccato notes.

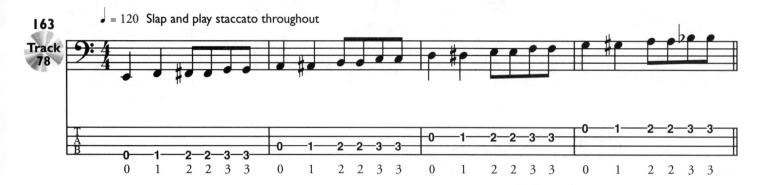

Popping

Popping notes goes right along with slapping. The act of popping requires you to hook your right-hand 1st or 2nd finger underneath the string, yank the string out as far as you can, and let it "thwack" right back into place. The string will slam into the fretboard, giving you a nice percussive sound (see photos to the right).

Preparing to pop.

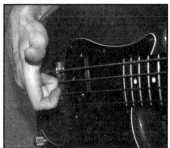

Follow-through of pop.

Slapping & popping work so well together because when you rotate your wrist preparing to slap or coming off of a slap, it is the same motion you should use for popping. Pops are notated by an uppercase P above the standard music notation.

Try popping each note up and down the major scale. First, play the exercise normally, giving each note its full value; then, practice it staccato.

P = Pop

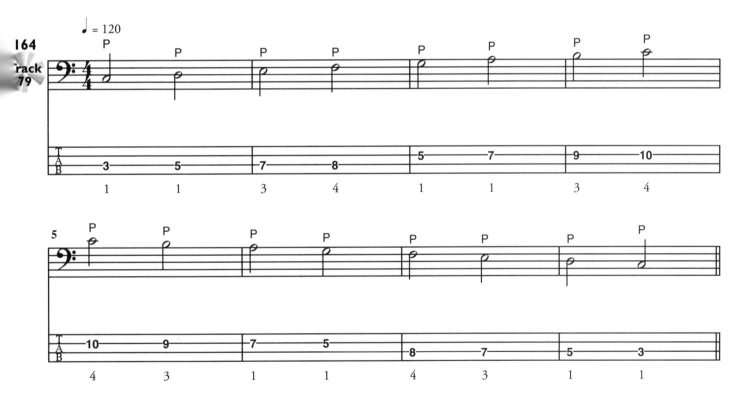

Slap & Pop Bass Lines

Following are some basic slap & pop exercises. In most cases, every slap will be followed by a pop. Remember to simply rotate the wrist and not actually pull the hand away from the strings.

This first bass line is a standard disco slap bass line. The octave is one of the most commonly used interval shapes when playing slap bass.

A great way to mix fluid and percussive sounds is to combine legato techniques such as slides, hammer-ons, and pull-offs with slapping & popping. Working in some dead, or muted, notes goes hand in hand with playing slap bass, because it adds even more to that percussive sound we're looking for.

Open-Hammer-Pop

A technique commonly used with slap bass is called the *open-hammer-pop*. This technique is simple, but has an advanced sound to it. You simply slap an open string, hammer-on to your target note, and then pop the third note of the pattern. Try out this technique with these next couple of bass lines.

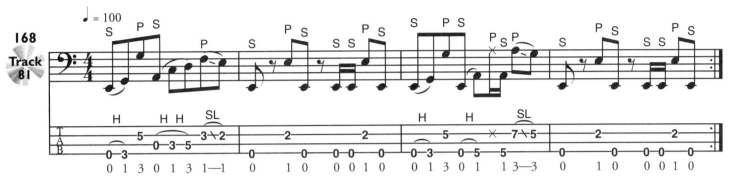

In the bass line below, you can see how effective the open-hammer-pop technique is for playing triplets. This bass line is in the style of Stevie Wonder's "Higher Ground," as performed by Flea and the Red Hot Chili Peppers. To execute slap & pop like Flea, you want to be sure to hold out the notes and let them ring, rather than to play them staccato (except where indicated).

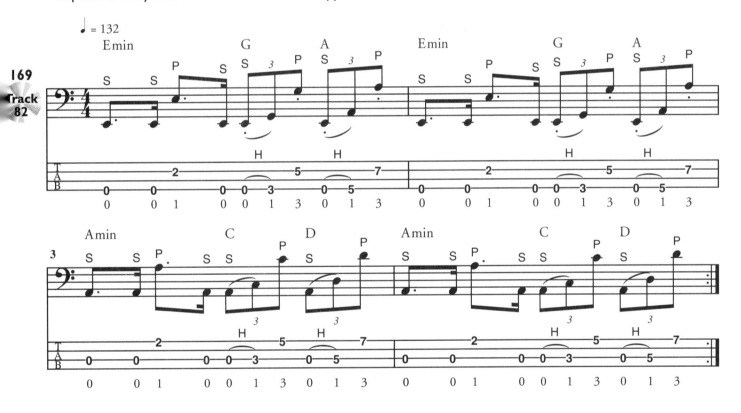

Try this bass line, which uses a *pop-and-pull-off-to-open-string* technique.

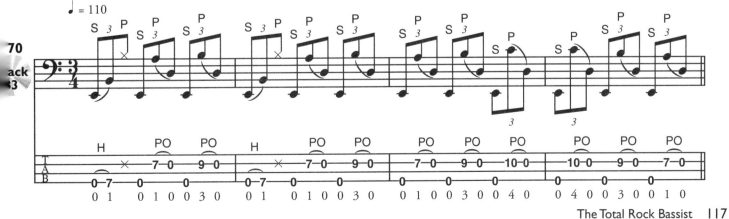

Slapping & Popping Double Stops

Another option we have is to combine slap bass with double-stops. Using the percussive slap & pop sounds over our beefy double-stops can thicken up our bass lines and really add some power to them.

Slapping double stops requires slightly changing the angle of the thumb to accommodate hitting both strings simultaneously; while popping two strings at the same time will require using both your 1st and 2nd right-hand fingers.

This first bass line will use pops to play the perfect 4th double stops. You may want to try barring your left-hand finger across both strings to play the double stops in this line.

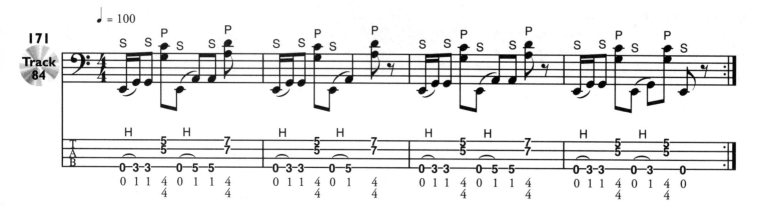

This bass line will have you slapping perfect 5th double stops on the top strings. Be sure to angle your thumb in order to slap both strings at the same time.

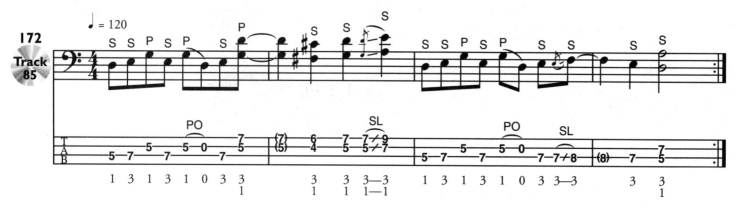

Chapter 13: Tapping

Tapping has become a much sought after technique among bass guitarists. Tapping involves playing notes on the fretboard using both your left and right hands. The act simply involves using both hands to perform hammer-ons; however to execute this technique efficiently, you need to develop good finger strength and dexterity.

The left-hand concept for tapping generally utilizes the strongest fingers, which most likely are your 1st and 2nd fingers. You will hammer-on from an open string, even though that open string may not necessarily be played (see photos below).

Preparing left-hand hammer-on.

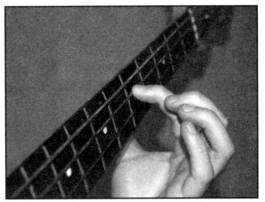

Completing left-hand hammer-on.

The right hand performs in a similar fashion. Your right arm will now be at a different angle, with your elbow near the bridge. Rather than having your fingers positioned perpendicularly to the strings as they normally would be, they will now be almost parallel to the strings.

When you hammer-on to the fretboard with the right hand, you want to make sure you keep your fingers curved, and that you hit the strings with a good amount of force to make the note ring out loud and clear. The tapping motion will mostly be coming from your wrist; you want to avoid pulling your entire arm far off the fretboard (see photos below).

Preparing to tap with your right hand.

Completing a right-hand tap.

Correct left- and right-hand tapping position.

Tapping Warm-Ups

Because tapping requires more strength than normal from both hands, it's important to get warmed up before getting too deeply into tapping exercises. These warm-ups start slowly and simply, and gradually build up speed. Remember, the goal now is to get the notes sounding as clear as possible. Something that can affect how well you'll be able to execute these tapping exercises is the *action* of the strings on the bass, which is how far your strings are from the fretboard. Lower action is recommended for well-executed tapping.

In this first warm-up, you will simply be tapping the interval of a major 3rd, using your left-hand 1st finger to play a C on the 8th fret of the 4th string, and your right-hand 1st finger to play an E on the 12th fret of the 4th string. Tapping is notated using the letters R and L

for right-hand and left-hand fingers, respectively. For example, R1 designates the 1st finger (index) of your right hand. You want to make sure that you keep your left-hand finger down before tapping with your right hand (the same concept used when playing normal hammer-ons with the left hand). Also, be sure to fully lift your right-hand finger off the fretboard before hammering-on with your left hand.

Once you are comfortable playing this exercise with your right-hand 1st finger, repeat it using your right-hand 2nd finger. If you are feeling ambitious, try playing this exercise with your 3rd and 4th right-hand fingers as well; they are used less for most common tapping practices, but it's always good to build strength wherever possible.

> R = Right-hand finger
> L = Left-hand finger

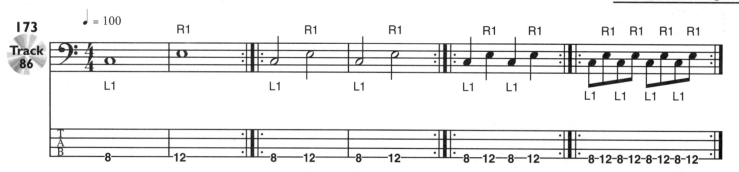

Now, try this tapping warm-up, which will take you across all four strings, and be sure to repeat it using your right-hand 2nd finger for tapping as well.

Tapping Exercises

The exercises below are designed to get your two right- and left-hand fingers tapping at the same time. This first one features major chord arpeggios ascending in whole steps, starting with G on the 3rd fret of the 4th string.

You will play the root and 3rd with your left-hand 1st and 2nd fingers, and then tap the 5th with your right-hand 1st finger, and the octave with your right-hand 2nd finger.

This next bass line keeps the 1st and 2nd right-hand fingers tapping on the 12th fret of the 2nd and 3rd strings, while the left hand moves up the 2nd string.

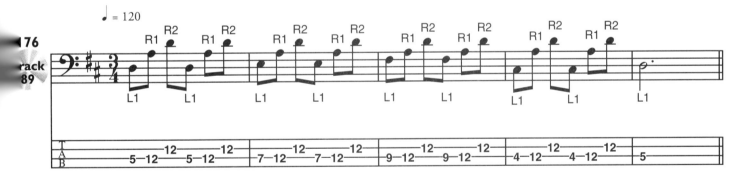

This is the same exercise as above, only played in eighth-note triplets.

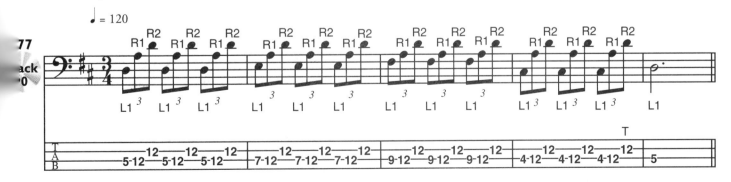

Tapping Bass Lines

This melodic bass line will have you tapping the same root and 5th on a D, while tapping and sliding around with your right-hand fingers. You can use whichever right-hand finger you choose, but it may be easiest and most beneficial for building strength to assign your 1st finger to the 2nd string and your 2nd finger to the 1st string.

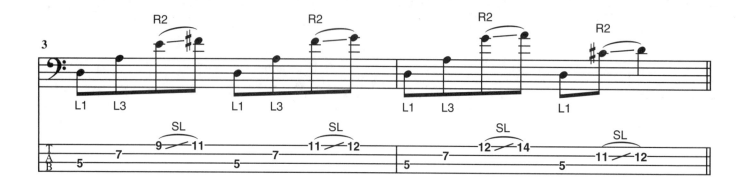

Tapping by itself can be used to create beautiful lines that are wonderful for solo bass parts. However, combining tapping with other techniques like slap bass or finger funk can get some amazing results. Les Claypool of Primus is a master of blending tapping in songs like "Tommy the Cat" and "Year of the Parrot."

This Primus-inspired bass line will have you playing normally for the first part of the bar, and then tapping and sliding double stops. For lines like this, it may help to play normally but move your right hand up closer to the fretboard.

This bass line mixes tapping and slap bass.

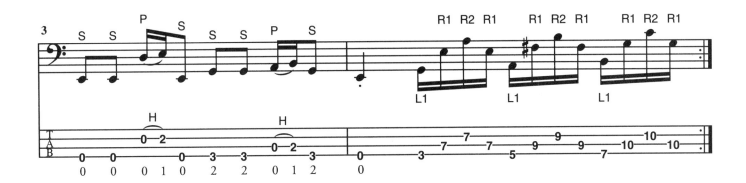

Rhythm Practice: Quarter-Note Triplets

Quarter-note triplets are tricky to read, but easy to feel. Just as eighth-note triplets resulted from breaking a quarter note into three parts, quarter-note triplets are the result of dividing a half note into three even parts. You will recognize a quarter-note triplet as three quarter notes with a bracket and a "3" over them.

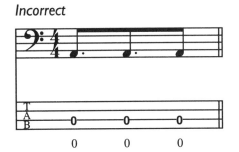

One common mistake people make when playing quarter-note triplets is to play them as two dotted eighth notes followed by an eighth note. This is incorrect, even though the feel is similar.

Incorrect

To properly understand how to play a quarter-note triplet, we can break it down using eighth-note triplets tied together.

Correct

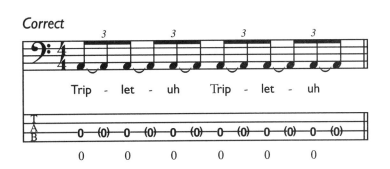

The following measure sounds the same as the measure of tied triplets on the previous page.

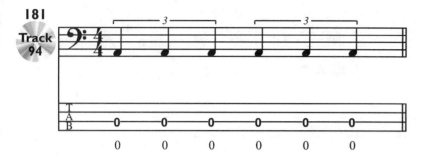

With these last few rhythmic exercises, be sure to take your time and get a grasp on the feel of the quarter-note triplet. This first one will only use half notes, quarter notes, and the quarter-note triplet.

This next one will add eighth notes to the mix.

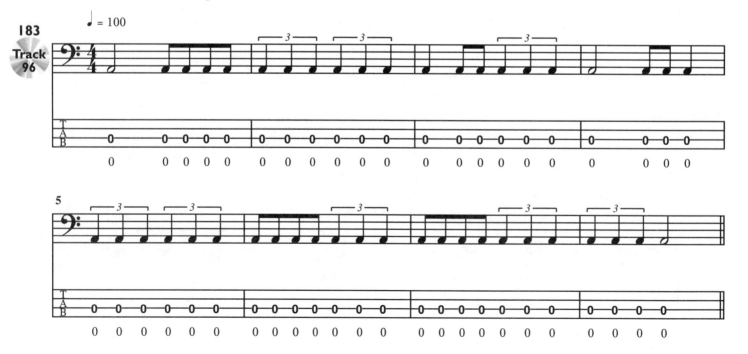

Now, we'll throw in some rests.

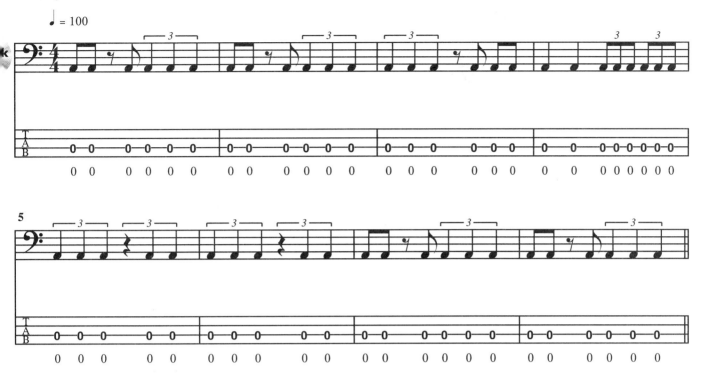

Quarter-Note Triplet Bass Lines

One common use of quarter-note triplets, especially in rock bass lines, is to signify the end of a phrase or a song, like in the following example. It is especially effective to use rhythms like this when the bass line consists of a steady rhythm.

Another common use of quarter-note triplets is to create *polyrhythmic contrast* between two instruments. When two different rhythms are played simultaneously, it is known as *polyrhythm*. In this example, the guitar is playing straight eighth notes throughout, but our bass line will chug on some tritone double stops, locking in with the drums in a quarter-note triplet rhythm every other measure. This technique is used a lot in modern day metal and hardcore songs.

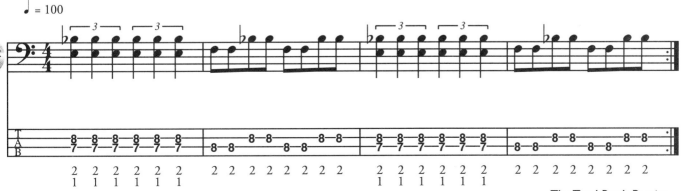

Appendix: Practice Tips

Be Organized

The best way to practice any instrument is to take a focused and organized approach. You want to manage your time evenly and consistently. Like preparing for a test, you'll retain information better reviewing it repeatedly over several practice sessions, rather than cramming all your practice time into one day.

Even if you have only 15 minutes to practice a day, this is much more effective than practicing for three hours straight, one day a week. It will not only help you to retain information and patterns better, but it will also help your muscles get used to the physical requirements of playing the bass.

A good approach to organizing your practice time is to list everything you want to focus on that week. Dedicate certain blocks of time to a variety of different subjects, making sure to be well rounded. Set up blocks of time to focus on things like rhythm exercises, scale exercises, reading exercises, learning new songs, and picking songs out by ear.

The Metronome Is Your Best Friend

Always use a metronome, click, or drum machine when practicing. As part of the rhythm section, it's the bassist's job to help keep time and groove. A bass player with a keen sense of time and rhythm is an invaluable asset to a band. Getting used to playing to a click will make your playing tighter and much more solid, and it will also help you to more easily recognize rhythmic patterns just from hearing them.

Being able to play to a click will also become very useful when playing live, and especially when recording. Laying down tracks in a studio is almost always done to a click to ensure the tightest performances, and being able to jump into a studio and play to a click will make everyone's life easier.

Play with Others

While practicing by yourself definitely has benefits and is essential to improving, nothing quite works better than playing with other musicians. Getting together with friends and jamming will you give a sense of your dynamic role as a bassist and will increase your creativity. The biggest benefit is that it's fun, which is one of the reasons we make music in the first place!

Playing live gigs is even more beneficial because it puts your skills to the test in a live environment. It may seem nerve-racking at first, but after that first gig, you'll feel the excitement that comes with playing live, and you are almost guaranteed to fall in love with the experience.

Listen, Listen, Listen

One of the best ways to improve technique on an instrument, as well as gain inspiration, is to listen to as much music as you can and focus in on the bass lines. Try finding transcriptions of the bass lines in books or magazines. There are many places to find free TAB online. These can be very helpful; however, these are often transcribed by amateurs and are inaccurate, as well as not providing any rhythm. So, the best approach to using untrustworthy internet TAB is to use the TAB only as a guide or starting point, and really listen and dig in to the song you are learning and try to figure out the absolute right way to play it.

Eventually, your ears will become more developed, and you'll recognize certain intervals and chords just from hearing them. This is an essential skill to have for playing with others and quickly writing bass lines. This skill will also help you to pick songs out by ear without the use of notation or TAB. You'll want to dig into some of your favorite songs and take them part by part, writing out the bass line as accurately as you can. This will also help to train your ear and recognize certain techniques as well. There are many techniques on the bass that have distinctive sounds, like slap & pop, hammer-ons, and tapping, which you will surely be able to hear in the music you listen to.

Observe

While listening to artists will surely help, it will also help to watch other musicians. Whether on a DVD, an Internet video, or even better, at a live concert, watching other musicians play will help you to develop your own playing techniques. Pay attention to how they hold the instrument, the sounds they are getting out of their live rig, and even how they interact with the audience and other band members. Musicians are unique people, and simply watching and taking mental notes can help you develop your own style.

Absorb

Another thing to do that will improve your playing is to absorb as much info as you can about your favorite artists. Bass magazines are always chock full of great articles that focus on everything from inspiration behind bass lines to gear profiles, and even include direct transcriptions. Even just reading an article on how a certain bassist approaches writing can inspire you and expand your creativity.

Conclusion

Congratulations on making it through this book! You should now have all the techniques and concepts needed to excel at playing rock bass. Now, it's time to expand your horizons and take on new genres and styles, or maybe create your own. There are no rules to music, and there is always something new to discover. Think about territories that haven't been explored yet, and who knows, maybe you'll be the next Larry Graham, Les Claypool, or Victor Wooten. Or, maybe you're content with just sitting back and feeling the groove, and that's just fine. There really is no wrong way to play rock bass. Good luck and have fun!